Global economic growth continued in 2011 as the world economy extended its recovery from the 2009 recession. During the 2012-21 projection period, income growth is projected to continue and be slightly above the historical average long-term rate during the last half of the period. This growth provides a foundation for gains in world demand and trade for agricultural products. Consequently, agricultural product prices are projected to remain historically high.

Historical Background for Trade Projections

Since early 2002, fluctuations in production, trade, and stocks of agricultural commodities have been unusually large, contributing to wide fluctuations in food commodity prices. Between January 2002 and June 2008, an index of monthly average world prices of wheat, rice, corn, and soybeans rose 226 percent and then declined 40 percent in the following 6 months. By June 2010, the index had fallen another 11 percent. The index then rose 70 percent by May 2011 and stood at double the January 2002 level, but 8 percent below the June 2008 peak. The 70-percent increase during the 11 months from June 2010 to May 2011 raised concerns about another food-commodity price spike of the magnitude experienced in 2007-08. Instead, after peaking in May 2011, the price index fell 11 percent by December 2011.

Monthly average crop prices 1/

Index values: January 2002 = 100

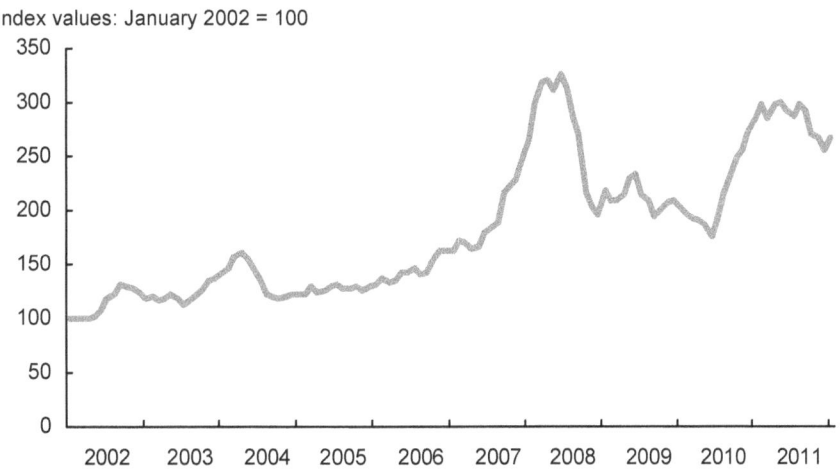

1/ ERS calculations based on International Monetary Fund (IMF) average monthly world price quotes for wheat, corn, soybeans, and rice; aggregated by IMF's fixed historical exports weights.

A series of adverse weather events were the main factors contributing to the increase in staple food prices from June 2010 to May 2011, beginning with a severe drought in Russia and parts of Ukraine and Kazakhstan that reduced production of all crops, but particularly wheat. In late summer 2010, yield prospects for U.S. corn declined due to high temperatures during pollination. About the same time, rain on the nearly mature wheat crops in Canada and northwestern Europe reduced a large portion of these crops to feed-grade quality. Continued drought in the former Soviet Union significantly reduced winter wheat plantings. After November 2010, drought and periodic high temperatures associated with a La Niña weather pattern reduced the corn and soybean crops in central Argentina. Rains in Australia in late 2010 to early 2011 downgraded much of the Australian wheat crop to feed quality, further reducing global supplies of food-quality wheat. In the southern Great Plains, drought persisted from fall 2010 through fall 2011 and reduced the region's harvests of hard red winter wheat, sorghum, corn and soybeans.

Other factors contributing to the rise in prices included continued global economic growth, especially in developing countries, the declining value of the U.S. dollar, and increasing energy prices.

Then, during the last half of 2011, crop prices declined 15 percent. High commodity prices in the fall of 2010 and first half of 2011 provided incentives for farmers in many parts of the world to increase their area planted. This, combined with more favorable global weather, contributed to an increase in world production and stocks of grains and oilseeds in 2011, despite a drop in U.S. corn yields. However, even with the projected increases in world crop production and stocks, world market prices are expected to remain well above historical levels for the next decade.

Trade Projections Overview

Developing countries are the main source of growth in world agricultural demand and trade. Food consumption and feed use are particularly responsive to income growth in developing countries, with movement away from staple and/or traditional foods and toward more diversified diets. Agricultural demand in developing countries is further reinforced by population growth rates that are about twice the average of developed countries.

General International Assumptions

Trade projections to 2021 are founded on assumptions concerning trends in foreign area, yields, and use as well as the assumption that countries comply with existing bilateral and multilateral agreements affecting agriculture and agricultural trade. The projections incorporate the effects of trade agreements and domestic policies in place or authorized by November 2011. International macroeconomic assumptions were completed in October 2011.

Domestic agricultural and trade policies in individual foreign countries are assumed to evolve along their current paths, based on the consensus judgment of USDA analysts. In particular, long-term economic and trade reforms in many developing countries are assumed to continue. Similarly, the development and use of technology and changes in consumer preferences are assumed to continue evolving based on past performance and analysts' judgments regarding future developments.

In particular, the combined region of Africa and the Middle East is projected to have some of the strongest growth in food demand and agricultural trade over the coming decade. Both poultry and beef imports have their largest projected increases in this region. By the end of the projection period, Africa and the Middle East are projected to account for about half of poultry imports and 22 percent of beef imports by the major importers of the world. Strong policy support for domestically produced meat also motivates growth in feed grain and protein meal imports, especially where land constraints or agroclimatic conditions limit an expansion of domestic crop production. As a result, the region accounts for about 23 percent of the projected growth in world coarse grain imports over the next 10 years. Strong import growth by Africa and the Middle East over the projection period also accounts for 48 percent of the increase in global wheat imports, 47 percent of the growth in rice imports, and 39 percent of the rise in soybean oil trade.

Mexico is projected to be another large growth market, not only for meat imports, but also for selected grains and oilseeds. A sustained increase in per capita Mexican meat demand over the next decade provides incentives to expand livestock production in that country as well as to import more meat. Imports of beef, pork, and poultry are projected to rise by 95, 42, and 28 percent, respectively. Mexico's increase in pork imports accounts for more than 11 percent of the growth in world pork trade. In addition, Mexico plays a dominant role in the world sorghum market, accounting for one-third of world imports and for more than 90 percent of the increase in world imports. For corn, Mexico is second only to China in projected import growth over the next 10 years.

Agricultural prices are projected to remain above pre-2006 levels during the coming decade as a result of several factors, including increasing world demand for grains, oilseeds, and livestock products; a depreciation of the U.S. dollar; continuing high energy prices; and some further growth in biofuels production.

Prices for vegetable oils are projected to rise relative to prices for protein meals. Oilseed prices rise slightly more than grain prices, and meat prices rise relative to the costs of feedstuffs, both for protein meals and grains.

World agricultural production rises in response to high prices and technology enhancements. However, a number of factors are expected to slow the rate of production growth. Many countries have a limited ability to expand planted area, and the expansion that does occur takes place on land with lower productive capacity. The growth rate in world-average crop yields has been slowing for nearly two decades, to some extent as a result of reduced research and development funding. Water constraints in some countries are impeding the expansion in irrigation. Where irrigation water is pumped from deep wells, the energy cost of pumping is projected to continue to increase. Costs of other production inputs such as fertilizers and chemicals are also likely to increase.

Traditional exporters of a wide range of agricultural products, such as Argentina, Australia, Canada, the European Union (EU), and the United States, remain important in global trade in the coming decade. But countries that have made significant investments in their agricultural sectors and increasingly pursuing policies intended to encourage agricultural production, including Brazil, Russia, Ukraine, and Kazakhstan, are expected to have an increasing presence in export markets for basic agricultural commodities.

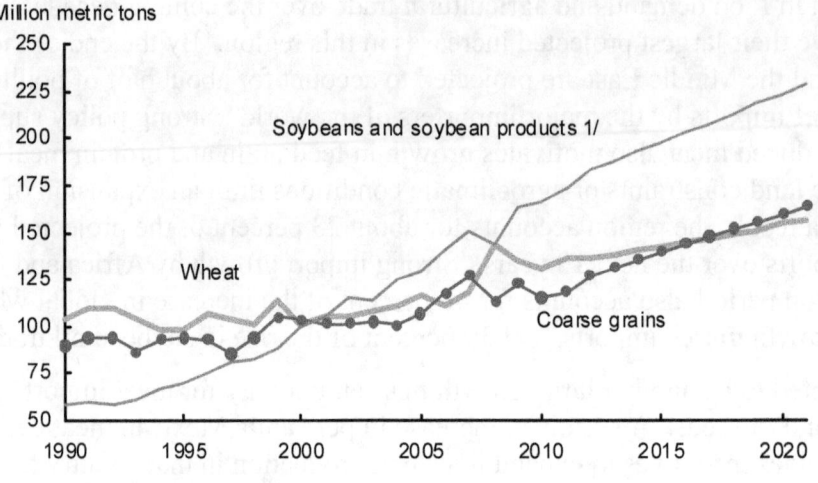

Global trade: Wheat, coarse grains, and soybeans and soybean products

Million metric tons

1/ Soybeans and soybean meal in soybean-equivalent units.

Global trade in soybeans and soybean products has risen rapidly since the early 1990s, and has surpassed global trade in wheat—the traditional leader in agricultural commodity trade—and in total coarse grains (corn, barley, sorghum, rye, oats, millet, and mixed grains). Continued strong growth in global demand for vegetable oil and protein meal, particularly in China and other Asian countries, is expected to maintain soybean and soybean-product trade well above wheat and coarse grains trade throughout the next decade.

- In most countries, the projected growth in total harvested area of all crops rises by less than 0.5 percent per year. Area expands more rapidly in countries with a reserve of available land and policies allow farmers to respond to higher prices. Such countries include Brazil, Russia, Ukraine, Argentina, and some other countries in South America and Eastern Europe. About two-thirds of the projected growth in global production is derived from rising yields, even though growth in crop yields is projected to slow.

- The market impact of slower yield growth is partially offset by slower growth in world population. Nonetheless, population growth is a significant factor driving overall growth in demand for agricultural products. Additionally, rising per capita income in many countries supplements population gains in the demand for vegetable oils, meats, horticultural products, and coarse grains. World per capita use of vegetable oils is projected to rise 15 percent over the next 10 years, compared with 6 percent for meat and for total coarse grains. Per capita use is projected to decline about 1 percent for wheat and rice.

- Increasing demand for wheat, coarse grains, oilseeds, and other crops provide incentives to expand global cultivated area and the intensity of cultivation. Higher prices for vegetable oils, as a result of increased demand for food use, biodiesel production, and other industrial uses, are bringing previously uncultivated land in Brazil, Argentina, Indonesia, and Malaysia into soybean and palm oil production. Globally, the area planted to total grains, oilseeds, and cotton is projected to expand about 0.75 percent per year.

- In the coming decade, the growth in global grain trade comes from a broad range of countries, but particularly from countries in Africa and the Middle East.

Demand for Biofuel Feedstocks

The demand for feedstocks currently used to produce ethanol and biodiesel is projected to continue growing in a number of countries—although at a slower pace than in recent years. Expansion continues to depend on policy support, mainly use mandates and tax incentives—motivated by environmental concerns and a goal to reduce energy dependence.

Six countries and regions (United States, Brazil, European Union (EU), Argentina, Canada, and China) accounted for about 90 percent of world biodiesel production and 97 percent of ethanol production in 2010. Their dominance in global biofuels markets is expected to change little in the coming decade. Between 2012 and 2021, production in these countries is projected to rise about 50 percent for biodiesel and 40 percent for ethanol.

Country Assumptions

EU. The EU is the world's third largest consumer and the largest importer of biofuels. Biodiesel production is projected to increase by one-third between 2012 and 2021. To boost biodiesel production, the EU increases oilseed production and imports of oilseeds and vegetable oil feedstocks, mainly from Ukraine and Russia. Biodiesel imports, mainly from Argentina, rise steadily. During the same period, fuel ethanol production is projected to increase about 75 percent. Internally produced wheat is the primary feedstock in the early years but the use of corn grows more rapidly toward the end of the projections. Ethanol imports, mainly from Brazil, are expected to increase. On a volume basis, ethanol's share of total biofuel use grows from about 30 percent currently, to 40 percent by 2021.

Brazil. In Brazil, the world's second largest biofuel producer, sugarcane-based ethanol production is projected to rebound from recently reduced levels that resulted from two years of low sugarcane production and high international sugar prices favoring the conversion of cane to sugar. Then from 2012 to 2021, Brazil's ethanol production is projected to rise more than 90 percent to meet both increasing domestic demand and growing export demand from Europe and the United States. Strong growth is also projected for soybean-oil-based biodiesel production, although rising from a much smaller base. Most of the biodiesel is used domestically.

Argentina. Argentina's biodiesel production is projected to expand 60 percent between 2012 and 2021. Although some of the biodiesel is used to meet a mandated increase in the domestic blend rate, exports continue to rise and the country maintains its position as the world's largest biodiesel exporter. Argentina's export tax structure favors exports of biodiesel rather than of soybean oil. Argentina's ethanol production increases at a faster rate than biodiesel production, but from a much smaller base.

Canada. Ethanol production is projected to increase 80 percent, with corn imports accounting for an increasing share of the feedstock. Biodiesel production climbs about 70 percent, most of it using rapeseed (canola) oil as a feedstock. Most of the increased biodiesel output is consumed in Canada, but limited amounts are exported to the United States and the EU. Some of the rapeseed-meal byproduct is exported to the United States.

China. About 4 million tons of corn were used to produce fuel ethanol in 2010. China has implemented policies to limit further expansion of grain- and oilseed-based biofuel production for transportation fuel use, and is now emphasizing the use of nongrain feedstocks such as cassava.

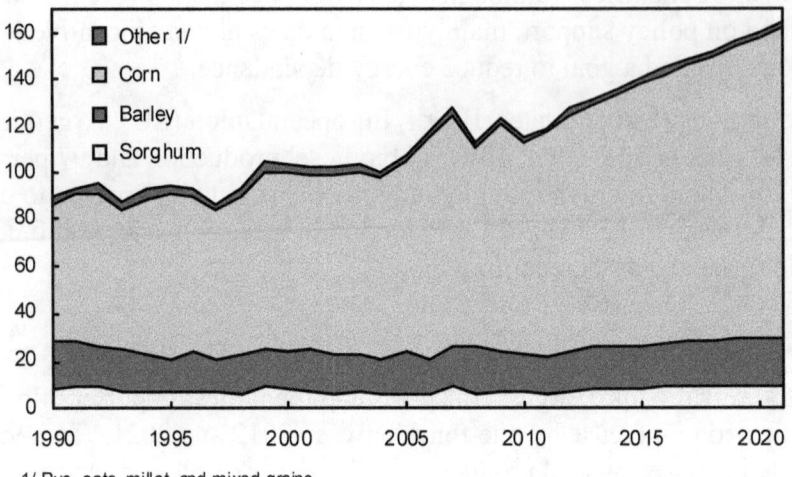

Global coarse grain trade

Million metric tons

Legend:
- Other 1/
- Corn
- Barley
- Sorghum

1/ Rye, oats, millet, and mixed grains.

World coarse grain trade expands 37 million metric tons (29 percent) from 2012 to 2021. The share of global coarse grain production used as animal feed trended downward from 66 percent a decade ago to about 57 percent in 2011 and is projected to remain just below 60 percent during the coming decade. Industrial uses, such as starch, ethanol, and malt production, are much smaller than feed use but are increasing twice as fast.

- Corn is the dominant feed grain traded in international markets. Corn's share of total world coarse grain trade continues to rise slowly and averages 80 percent through the projection period. Barley has the next largest share (13 percent), followed by sorghum (5 percent). The trade share of the other coarse grains, mostly oats and rye, continues to decline slowly to about 2 percent by 2021.

- Corn's increasing share of world production and trade of coarse grains is attributable to yield growth that is more rapid than for other grains, to new varieties that enable it to be competitive in a wider range of climatic regions, and to its preferred qualities for feed, biofuels, and other industrial uses. Average world corn yields are projected to trend upwards 1 percent a year while barley and sorghum yields both increase less than two-thirds of a percent a year.

- Commercialization of livestock feeding has been a driving force behind the growing dominance of corn in international feed grain markets. Hogs and ruminants, such as cattle and sheep, are capable of digesting a broad range of feedstuffs, making demand relatively price-sensitive across alternate feed sources. However, as pork and poultry production becomes increasingly commercialized throughout the world, higher quality feeds are used, boosting the demand for corn and soybean meal.

- The expansion of livestock production in feed-deficit countries has also contributed to the growth in coarse grain trade. Such countries are most often found in the Middle East, North Africa, and Asia.

Global coarse grain imports

Million metric tons

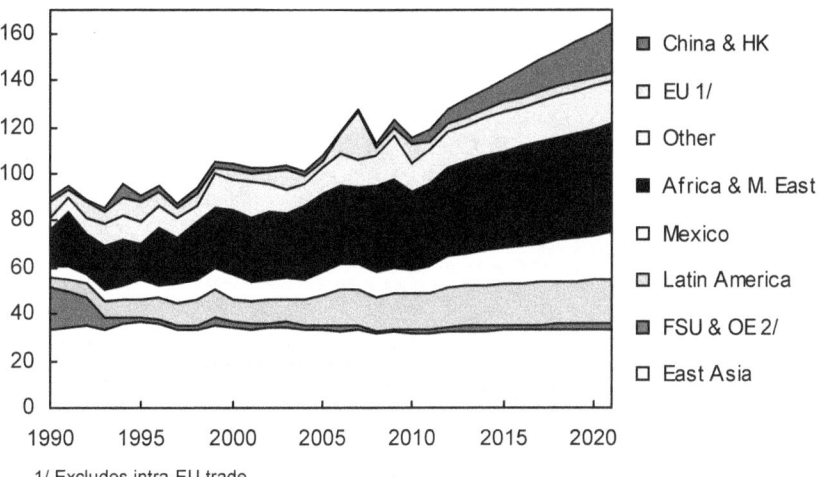

1/ Excludes intra-EU trade.
2/ Former Soviet Union and other Europe; prior to 1999, includes Czech Republic,
Estonia, Hungary, Latvia, Lithuania, Malta, Poland, Slovakia, and Slovenia.

World corn trade is projected to increases 31 million metric tons (31 percent) to 131 million tons between 2012/13 and 2021/22.

- Growth in coarse grain imports is strongly linked to expansion of livestock production in regions unable to meet their own feed needs. Key growth markets include North Africa, the Middle East, China, Mexico, and Southeast Asia. Japan and South Korea are large but mature markets for coarse grain imports.

- China's net imports of corn are projected to reach 18 million tons by the end of the projection period as imports grow steadily while exports remain small. China's strengthening domestic demand for corn is driven by its expanding livestock and industrial sectors. The increase in China's imports accounts for 45 percent of the 2012/13 to 2021/22 growth in world corn trade.

- Coarse grain imports by Africa and the Middle East account for more than 25 percent of the growth in world trade through 2021 as rising populations and increasing incomes sustain strong demand growth for animal products.

- Mexico's corn imports are projected to rise from 9.8 million tons in 2011/12 to nearly 16 million in 2021/22. Mexico's sorghum imports rise rapidly from reduced levels in recent years to 4.2 million tons by 2021/22. Altogether, the growth in Mexico's coarse grain imports represents almost one-fifth of the increase in global coarse grain trade during the coming decade. This reflects increased meat consumption in Mexican diets that stimulates an expansion in domestic meat production as well as increased meat imports.

- South and Southeast Asian corn imports rise 3 million tons (39 percent) by 2021 in response to increased demand from livestock producers. The region accounts for 10 percent of the growth in world corn imports.

- In East Asia (Japan, South Korea, Taiwan, and Hong Kong), imports of coarse grains grow very little because environmental constraints on expanding livestock production and increasing imports of selected cuts of meat greatly limit the growth in coarse grain imports.

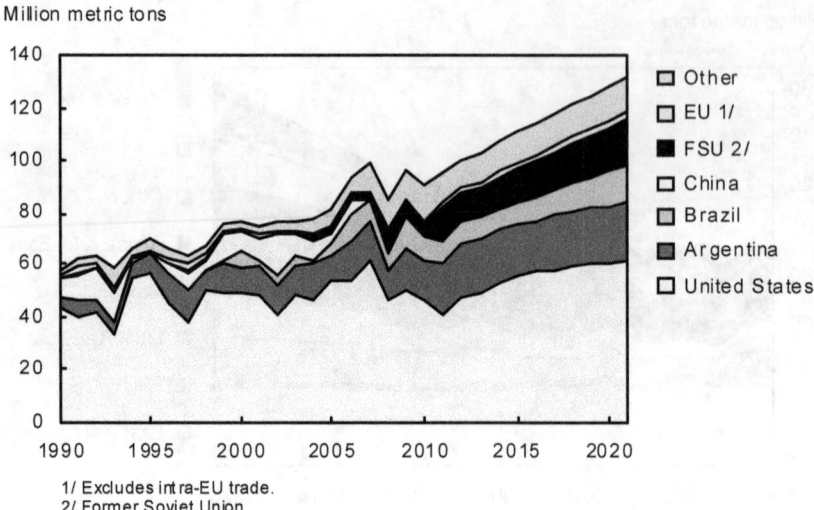

Global corn exports

Million metric tons

1/ Excludes intra-EU trade.
2/ Former Soviet Union.

U.S. corn exports are projected to grow over the next decade and approach record levels by 2021. However, large world supplies of feed-quality wheat compete with U.S. corn exports at the beginning of the projection period. The U.S. share of world corn trade declines slowly from an average of about 55 percent during the last half decade to less than 47 percent by 2021 as exports rise more rapidly from the countries of the former Soviet Union (FSU), Brazil, the EU, and other European countries.

- Corn exports from the FSU, mostly Ukraine, rise nearly 60 percent to more than 17 million tons by 2021. Favorable resource endowments, increasing economic openness, wider use of hybrid seed, and greater investment in agriculture all stimulate corn production in this region.

- Brazilian production and exports of corn are projected to increase in response to high world prices, especially during the latter part of the projection period. Brazil's corn exports have been large during the last few years as Brazil has targeted the EU's demand for grain that is not genetically modified (GM). This marketing opportunity has diminished as Brazil has expanded its own production of GM corn varieties.

- Argentina's corn area and exports are projected to stagnate in the early years of the projections due to the continuation of quantitative controls on exports. Then, exports grow slowly toward the end of the period. Still, with a small domestic market for corn, Argentina remains the world's second-largest corn exporter.

- Increases in corn area and yields enable the EU to increase production. Although the EU allocates more corn to fuel ethanol production, its exports increase and imports decline in the projections. The eastern part of the EU has a transportation advantage to parts of North Africa and the Middle East. Corn exports by other European countries, mostly Serbia, are also projected to rise.

Global barley imports

Million metric tons

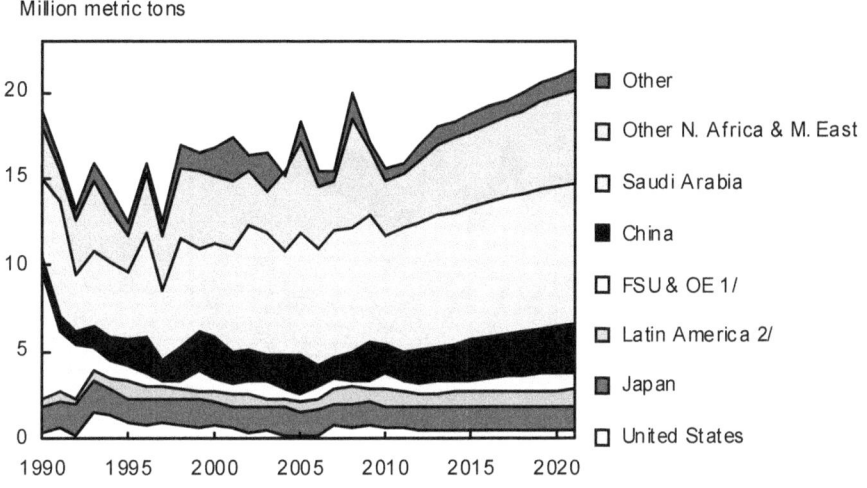

1/ Former Soviet Union and other Europe; prior to 1999, includes Czech Republic, Estonia, Hungary, Latvia, Lithuania, Malta, Poland, Slovakia, and Slovenia.
2/ Includes Mexico.

Global barley trade expands 4.3 million tons (25 percent) during the projection period. Rising demand for both malting and feed barley underpins the increased trade.

- Feed barley imports by the North African and Middle Eastern countries grow steadily over the next decade. This region is projected to account for 60 percent of the growth in world imports during the coming decade, and by 2021 they are projected to account for 65 percent of total world imports. During the mid-1990s, corn overtook barley as the principal coarse grain imported by these countries, due mainly to rising poultry production. Now, barley imports are rising more rapidly than imports of corn.

- Saudi Arabia remains by far the world's leading importer of barley, accounting for about 40 percent of world imports. However, its share declines during the projections as the barley imports of many other countries climb at a faster rate. Saudi Arabia's barley imports are used primarily as feed for sheep, goats, and camels.

- Among countries in the Middle East, Iran's barley imports are projected to experience the fastest growth rate over the next decade. Total imports by other countries in North Africa and the Middle East are projected to grow more slowly, but still account for about a fourth of the increase in world barley trade.

- The international market for malting barley is boosted by strong growth in beer demand in some developing countries, most notably in China—the world's largest malting-barley importer. China's domestic malting-barley production is increasing, but imports also rise during the projection period. Australia and Canada are China's main sources of malting barley imports.

Global barley exports

Million metric tons

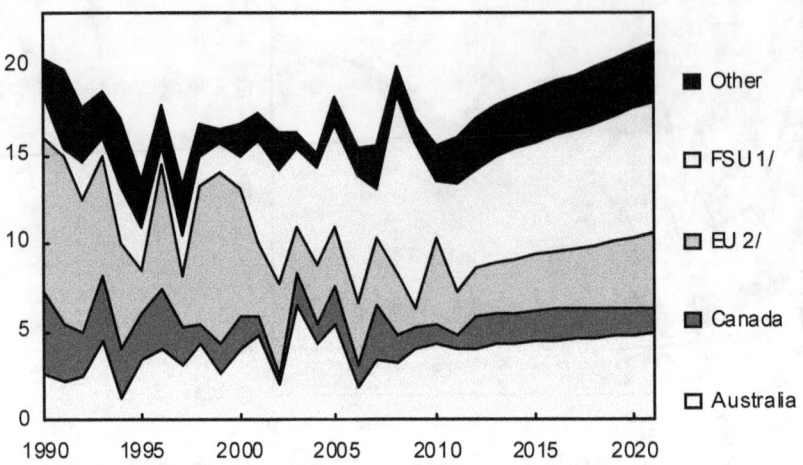

1/ Former Soviet Union and other Europe; prior to 1999, includes Czech Republic, Estonia, Hungary, Latvia, Lithuania, Malta, Poland, Slovakia, and Slovenia.
2/ Excludes intra-EU trade.

Ukraine became the world's largest barley exporter in 2009 and is expected to remain so throughout the 2012/13 to 2021/22 projection period. Australia, the EU, and Canada are expected to continue to be major exporters.

- Barley exports by the FSU are projected to reach 7.4 million tons by 2021 with Ukraine accounting for 5.1 million tons and Russia accounting for 1.0 million tons. This region's exports are projected to account for 44 percent of the increase in world exports over the next decade.

- Australia's barley exports are projected to rise slowly, and the country becomes the world's second-largest exporter, surpassing the EU.

- The EU's barley exports are projected to climb modestly during the coming decade, but remain well below the levels of the late 1990s.

- Malting barley commands a substantial price premium over feed barley. This quality premium is expected to influence planting decisions in Canada and Australia where malting barley's share of total barley area is expected to rise during the next 10 years. However, Canada's total area planted to all barley continues to decline gradually as canola remains more profitable. All of Ukraine's exports are feed-quality barley.

Global sorghum imports

Million metric tons

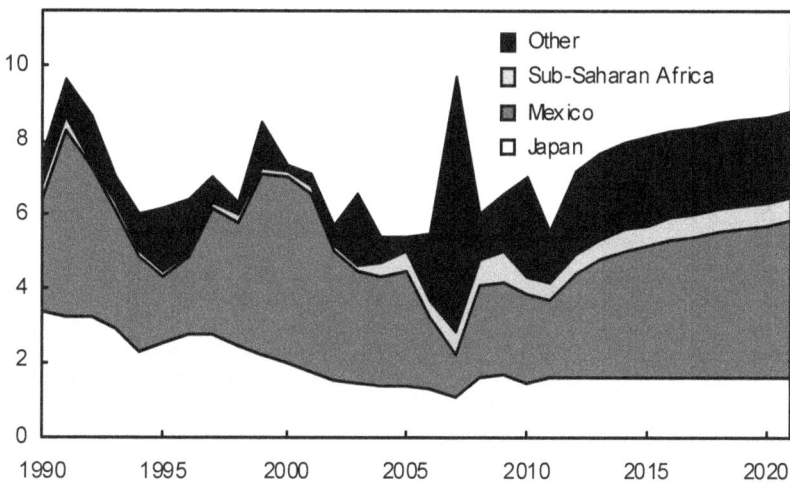

World sorghum trade is projected to trend upward from around 6.5 million tons in recent years to 8.8 million tons by 2021. U.S. sorghum exports to Mexico and Japan account for the bulk of world sorghum trade.

- U.S. sorghum exports are projected to recover from the current year low through 2013/14, then to remain flat at 4.3 million tons through 2021/22. These levels are still well below historical highs. Nevertheless, the United States is projected to remain the leading sorghum exporter throughout the period.

- Both Argentina and Australia—the world's second- and third-largest exporters—are expected to continue being prominent exporters during the coming decade. Argentina's exports are projected to rise about 60 percent to 3.5 million tons, while Australia's exports are projected to remain in the neighborhood of 0.6 million tons. Argentina's production and exports of new sorghum varieties with lower tannin content enable it to gain a larger share of the international market. The primary sorghum markets for Argentina are Japan, Chile, and Europe.

- Mexico's sorghum imports are projected to nearly double to 4.2 million tons by 2021. Many Mexican livestock producers have a slight preference for feeding sorghum, while U.S. livestock feeders increasingly prefer corn, thus facilitating U.S. sorghum shipments to Mexico. Mexico generally accounts for 30-40 percent of world sorghum imports but its share rises to nearly 50 percent by 2021.

- Sorghum imports by Japan—the world's second-largest importer—have trended slowly downward during the past decade. After a small rebound since 2007/08, imports are projected to remain stable over the next decade.

- Sub-Saharan Africa is the only other major export destination whose sorghum imports are projected to grow during the coming decade, and that projected growth is small.

Global wheat imports

Million metric tons

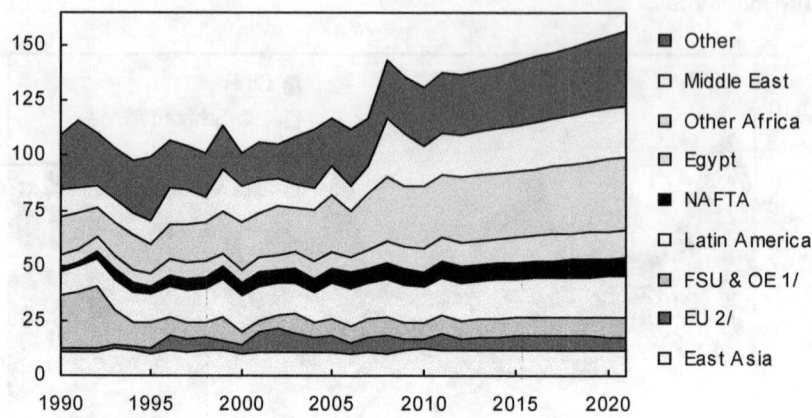

1/ Former Soviet Union and other Europe; prior to 1999, includes Czech Republic, Estonia, Hungary, Latvia, Lithuania, Malta, Poland, Slovakia, and Slovenia.
2/ Excludes intra-EU trade.

World wheat trade (including flour) expands by 20 million tons (15 percent) between 2012 and 2021, rising to nearly 157 million tons. Growth in wheat imports is concentrated in those developing countries where income and population gains drive increases in demand. The largest growth markets include Asian countries, the 15 countries of the Economic Community of West African States, other Sub-Saharan Africa countries, Egypt, Indonesia, Saudi Arabia, and other countries in the Africa and Middle East region.

- In many developing countries, almost no change in per capita wheat consumption is expected, but imports are projected to expand modestly because of population growth and limited potential to expand domestic wheat production. As incomes rise in Indonesia, Vietnam, and some other Asian countries, consumers shift marginally from rice to wheat. Nonetheless, overall global per capita wheat consumption is projected to decline slightly during the coming decade.

- Egypt maintains its position as the world's largest wheat-importing country, as its imports climb to more than 12 million tons. Imports by the EU, Brazil, and Indonesia are each projected to exceed 6 million tons by 2021.

- Imports by countries in Africa and the Middle East rise more than 9 million tons and account for 48 percent of the total increase in world wheat trade. Saudi Arabia has adopted a policy to phase out wheat production by 2016 because of water scarcity concerns, and imports are projected to rise to more than 3 million tons by 2021.

- China's imports remain small as per capita consumption of wheat continues to decline.

- EU wheat is the main feedstock used to produce fuel ethanol during the next several years. Then, the feedstock use shifts to corn to support further expansion in ethanol production.

- Abundant quantities of feed-quality wheat in a number of countries enable wheat to compete effectively with corn for feed use for the next couple of years. Europe has accounted for 45 to 53 percent of global wheat feeding during the past decade. However, its share declines to 40 percent by 2021 as wheat feeding expands in other countries in response to lower prices of wheat relative to coarse grains.

Global wheat exports

Million metric tons

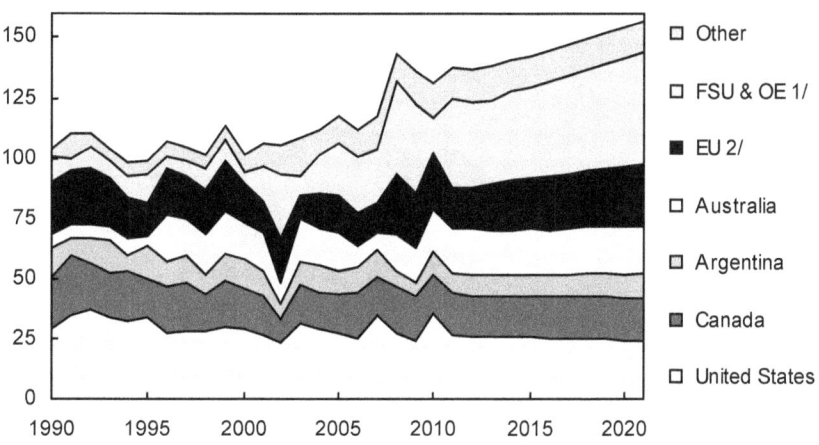

1/ Former Soviet Union and other Europe; prior to 1999, includes Czech Republic, Estonia, Hungary, Latvia, Lithuania, Malta, Poland, Slovakia, and Slovenia.
2/ Excludes intra-EU trade.

The traditional five largest wheat exporters (the United States, Australia, the EU, Argentina, and Canada) are projected to account for almost 62 percent of world trade in 2021, compared with 69 percent during the last decade. This decrease in share is mostly due to increased exports from the Black Sea area.

- Net U.S. wheat exports decline from 22.8 million tons at the beginning of the projection period to 21.0 million tons at the end. U.S. wheat exports are projected to account for less than 16 percent of global wheat trade at the end of the projection period, down from about 23 percent in the past 5 years.

- Argentina and the EU are the only traditional exporters whose market shares are projected to increase. Shares of world wheat exports increase for Russia, Ukraine, and Kazakhstan.

- Russia, Ukraine, and Kazakhstan became significant wheat exporters during the last half decade until the 2010 drought reduced production and exports. Exports from these countries are expected to recover in the coming years and to account for about 30 percent of world exports by 2021. Increasing wheat use for domestic feed is expected to prevent even more rapid export growth. Although not assumed, year-to-year volatility in production and trade is likely sometime in the projection period because of the region's highly variable weather and yields.

- EU wheat exports climb over the next decade as ethanol production shifts to increased use of corn and feed use trends slowly downward. After dropping sharply in 2011 and 2012, EU wheat exports are projected to trend upward and reach 26 million tons by 2021, well above the levels of the last decade.

- Canada's wheat area continues to decline slowly in response to increased global demand for vegetable oils (especially rapeseed oil) and for barley. As a result, little change is projected for Canadian wheat exports. The Canadian Wheat Board is assumed to function as in the past.

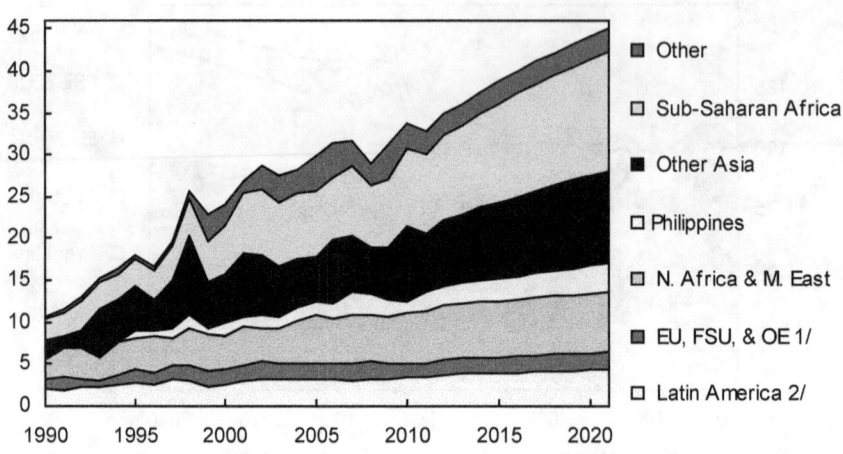

Global rice imports

Million metric tons

Legend:
- Other
- Sub-Saharan Africa
- Other Asia
- Philippines
- N. Africa & M. East
- EU, FSU, & OE 1/
- Latin America 2/

1/ European Union, former Soviet Union, and other Europe. 2/ Includes Mexico.

Global rice trade is projected to grow 2.9 percent per year from 2012 to 2021. In 2021, global rice trade reaches 45 million tons, 42 percent above the 2007 record. The main factors driving this expansion in global trade are a steady growth in demand—largely due to population growth in developing countries—and the inability of several key importers to significantly boost production. World trade as a share of world consumption, currently about 7 percent, remains substantially smaller than for other grains and oilseeds.

- Long-grain varieties account for around three-fourths of global rice trade and are expected to account for the bulk of trade growth over the next decade. Medium- and short-grain varieties account for 10 to 12 percent of global trade, with Northeast Asia the largest market. Aromatic rice, primarily basmati and jasmine, makes up most of the rest of global rice trade.

- In Africa and the Middle East, strong demand growth is driven by rapidly expanding population and income, while production growth is limited. In North Africa and the Middle East, production is primarily limited by climate. In Sub-Saharan Africa, expanding production is constrained by infrastructure deficiencies and resource constraints. Altogether, the entire Africa and Middle East region accounts for nearly half of the increase in world rice trade between 2012 and 2021. Africa accounts for most of this region's rising imports.

- The Philippines and Indonesia become the largest individual rice-importing countries by the end of the projection period. By 2021, each country is projected to import 3.3 million tons of rice or more. Other major importers—the EU, Iraq, Iran, Saudi Arabia, and Bangladesh—each take more than 1.3 million tons. These countries have limited ability to expand rice production and are expected to account for more than one-third of the increase in global rice imports over the next decade.

- Rice imports by the Central America and Caribbean region are projected to increase by 0.3 million tons over the next decade and to surpass 2 million by 2021. Population growth and rising per capita incomes boost rice consumption and raise imports in this region.

- In the EU, Canada, and the United States, immigration is the driving force for rising per capita consumption and modest import growth. In Mexico, higher incomes contribute to higher per capita consumption and moderate gains in imports.

- Imports by the FSU are projected to remain stable as a result of strong production growth and declining population that more than offsets slowly rising per capita consumption.

Global rice exports

Million metric tons

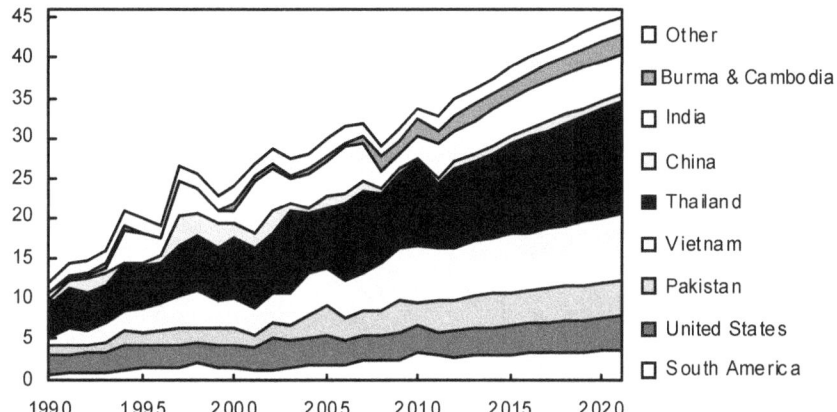

Asia continues to supply most of the world's rice exports throughout the projection period.

- Rice exports from Thailand and Vietnam, the world's largest rice-exporting countries, account for more than 45 percent of world trade and for more than 50 percent of the growth in world exports in the coming decade. Thailand's exports increase 4.1 million tons, to more than 14 million by 2021. Rice area and yields are projected to increase in Thailand. Vietnam's export expansion is smaller, rising from 6.5 to 8.1 million tons. Per capita consumption declines slowly for both exporters as incomes rise.

- India has typically been the third- or fourth-largest rice exporter since the mid-1990s, but its export levels have been volatile, primarily due to fluctuating stock levels and Government policies. India's exports have been well below previous levels for the last several years as exports of non-basmati rice have largely been banned since the spike in world prices in early 2008. In September 2011, the Government eased this ban. India's rice exports are projected to rise to about 4.8 million tons by 2021, making it the third-largest exporter.

- Pakistan and the United States have each been exporting around 3.5 million tons in recent years. Both exporters are projected to raise their exports to above 4 million tons over the next decade. Pakistan has expanded its rice area and production in recent years although production declined in 2010 due to devastating floods. In the coming decade, Pakistan's agricultural sector will be confronted by a growing water shortage and a deteriorating infrastructure, limiting production and export gains.

- U.S. expansion in rice exports is attributable to a slight area expansion after 2012, continued yield growth, and only modest growth in domestic use.

- Rice exports from China, the sixth-largest rice-exporting country, have declined in recent years but are projected to begin rising again and to reach 1.2 million tons by 2021, about double the level shipped in recent years. Little change in production or total disappearance is expected. Higher yields are projected to offset declining area as China allows the use of genetically modified rice. Reductions in per capita consumption, a result of continued diet diversification resulting from higher incomes, are expected to offset population growth. China also builds rice stocks during the projection period.

- Australian exports are projected to recover only modestly from the extremely low levels shipped during much of the past decade. Exports will continue to be limited by competing demands for irrigation water.

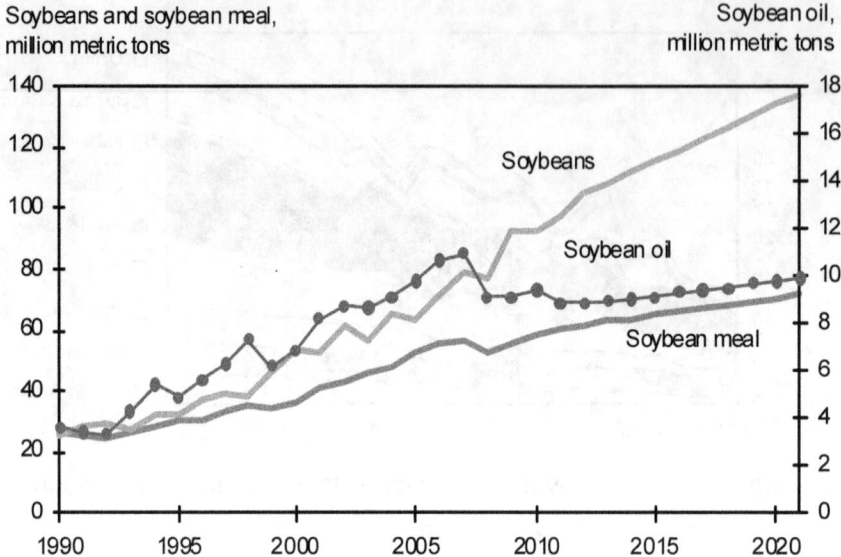

Global exports: Soybeans, soybean meal, and soybean oil

Economic growth and population increases in developing countries are projected to boost demand for vegetable oils for food consumption and for protein meals used in livestock production. Vegetable oil used for biodiesel production also is projected to increase. With demand for vegetable oils increasing at a faster rate than for protein meals, prices rise more rapidly for vegetable oils than for oilseeds and protein meals, particularly for rapeseed oil compared with rapeseed meal.

- Many countries with limited opportunity to expand oilseed production, such as China and some countries in North Africa, the Middle East, and South Asia, have invested heavily in crushing capacity in recent years. As a result, their import demand for oilseeds has grown rapidly and this growth is projected to continue. During the next decade, global trade in soybeans is projected to increase by 31 percent, soybean meal by 17 percent, and soybean oil by 12 percent.

- In China, per capita income is projected to continue rising rapidly thereby expanding consumer demand for livestock products and vegetable oils. Feed rations are expected to include an increasing percentage of protein meal to improve rates of weight gain for meat-producing animals. China mostly will import oilseeds for crushing rather than large amounts of oilseed meals and oils. This affects the composition of world trade by raising global import demand for oilseeds rather than for oilseed products.

- Argentina, Brazil, and the United States continue to account for about 88 percent of the world's aggregate exports of soybeans, soybean meal, and soybean oil during the coming decade. In Argentina, uncertainties about grain policies cause farmers to keep more land in soybean production. Also, some pasture land is shifted to soybean cultivation. Argentina's share of world exports of soybeans and soybean products remains about 27 percent. Brazil's soybean area continues to increase, but an increasing share of soybean production is crushed for domestic feed and food use. Brazil's share of world exports of soybeans and soybean products remains in the 32-36 percent range, while the U.S. share declines from just above 30 percent to about 25 percent by 2021.

- The EU is expected to expand biodiesel production using rapeseed oil as the primary feedstock. Rapeseed area increases early in the projections. Although EU imports of soybeans are projected to decline, imports of soybean meal and soybean oil are projected to increase.

Global soybean imports

Million metric tons

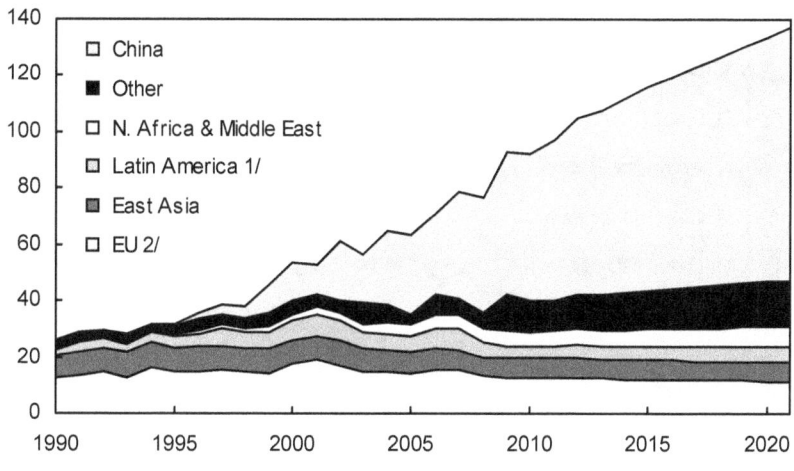

1/ Includes Mexico. 2/ Excludes intra-EU trade.

World soybean trade is projected to rise rapidly, but at a slower pace than in recent years, climbing nearly 32 million tons (nearly 31 percent) to 137 million tons during the next decade.

- China's soybean imports have risen sharply and now account for more than half of world trade. Over the coming decade, China will face policy decisions regarding the tradeoffs between producing and importing corn and soybeans. The projections assume that Chinese policies will pursue increasing corn production and letting soybean imports increase. Thus, China soybean imports are projected to rise 59 percent to 90 million tons in 2021/22 and to account for more than 80 percent of the projected growth in global soybean imports. China's underutilized oilseed crushing capacity drives strong gains in soybean imports but the use of vegetable oils for biodiesel production is assumed to have a negligible impact on the country's total vegetable oil use.

- EU soybean imports declined over the past decade due to decreases in internal grain prices, increases in grain and rapeseed meal feeding, and rising imports of soybean meal. These trends are projected to continue with imports falling 9 percent to 11.5 million tons.

- Imports of soybeans and soymeal by East Asia (Japan, South Korea, and Taiwan) are influenced by a continuing shift from importing feedstuffs to importing meat and other livestock products. As a result, this region's projected soybean imports decline slightly. Small increases in soymeal imports support slowly rising meat production in this region..

- Mexico's soybean imports are projected to increase more than 22 percent to 4.3 million tons. These imports will support the production of soybean meal for the Mexican poultry and pork industries and soybean oil for domestic food consumption.

- Egypt, Iran, and Turkey are projected to increase soybean imports in an effort to improve feed rations and meet increased per capita demand for vegetable oil consumption. These countries have a limited ability to expand their soybean production.

Global soybean exports

Million metric tons

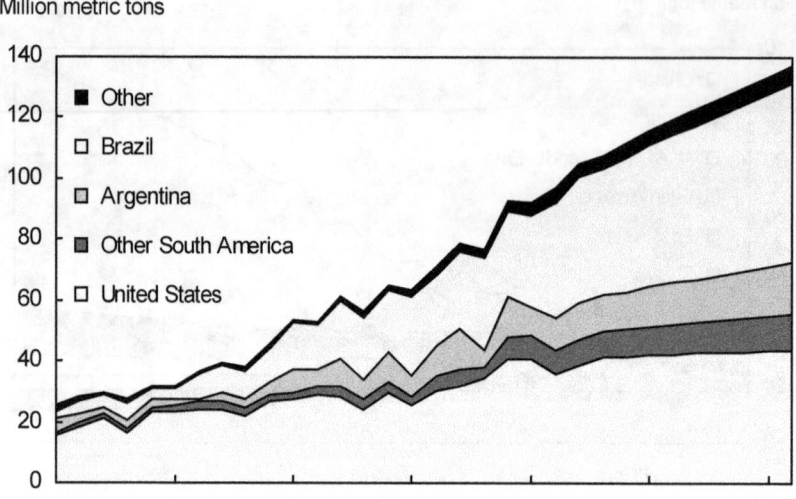

The three leading soybean exporters—the United States, Brazil, and Argentina—accounted for slightly more than 90 percent of world trade prior to 2009/10. Since then, exports from Uruguay, Paraguay, Bolivia, and other countries have increased; a trend that is expected to continue during the coming decade. However, the share held by the traditional exporters only slips to 87 percent.

- Brazilian soybean exports are projected to rise 18 million tons (43 percent) to 59.2 million tons during the 2012/13 to 2021/22 projection period, enabling the country to strengthen its position as the world's leading exporter of soybeans and soybean products. As world oilseed prices rise relative to grain prices, soybeans remain more profitable than other crops in most areas of Brazil. With increasing soybean plantings in the Cerrado region and expansion extending into the region defined as the "Amazon Legal," the increase in area planted to soybeans is projected to average about 2 percent per year during the coming decade.

- Argentina's export tax rates are higher for soybeans than for soybean products, a policy that favors domestic crushing of whole seeds and exporting of the products. However, in response to world demand for soybeans for crushing, Argentina's soybean exports have risen sharply and are projected to continue doing so, rising about 38 percent to nearly 17 million tons by 2021/22. Most of the soybeans exported by Argentina go to China.

- Other South American countries, principally Uruguay, Paraguay, and Bolivia, respond to higher oilseed prices by expanding the area planted to soybeans. Exports by these countries increase 50 percent to nearly 12 million tons.

- Although Ukraine's soybean exports are small, the country is expected to respond to higher international market prices for oilseeds by increasing production of rapeseed and soybeans. Ukraine's soybean exports are projected to rise 40 percent to 2 million tons by 2021/22.

Global soybean meal imports

Million metric tons

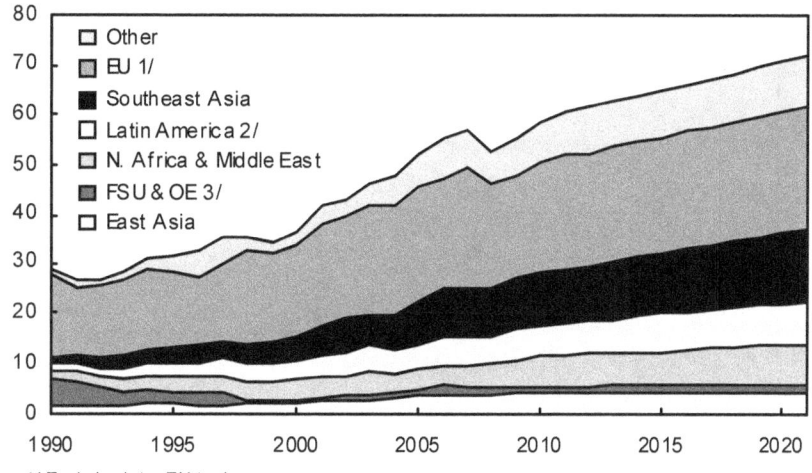

Legend:
- □ Other
- ▨ EU 1/
- ■ Southeast Asia
- □ Latin America 2/
- □ N. Africa & Middle East
- ▨ FSU & OE 3/
- □ East Asia

1/ Excludes intra-EU trade.
2/ Includes Mexico. 3/ Former Soviet Union and other Europe; prior to 1999, includes Czech Republic, Estonia, Hungary, Latvia, Lithuania, Malta, Poland, Slovakia, and Slovenia.

World soybean meal trade is projected to climb by more than 10 million tons (17 percent) to 71.9 million tons by 2021/22. In a number of countries with rising middle-income populations, continued growth in the demand for livestock products, limited capability to increase domestic oilseed production, and relatively lower world prices for protein meals boost soybean meal demand. Lower import prices for soybean meal relative to soybeans and grains provide incentives to use soybean meal at a higher rate in livestock feed rations.

- The EU remains the world's largest soybean-meal importer throughout the projections, despite increased domestic feeding of grains and rapeseed meal. Although abundant supplies of low-cost rapeseed meal are expected to be available as a result of expanded EU biodiesel production, there are technical limits on how much rapeseed meal can be incorporated in livestock rations. As a result, slow growth in EU soybean meal imports is expected to continue.

- The regions of Southeast Asia, Latin America, North Africa, and the Middle East become larger importers of soybean meal due to increasing demand for livestock feed and low oilseed meal prices. Imports by Southeast Asia, especially Vietnam, climb rapidly and account for one-third of the projected increase in world soymeal trade. Imports by countries in North Africa and the Middle East are projected to rise 1.5 million tons, and account for 15 percent of the increase in world trade. Although Latin America's soymeal imports increase by 2 million tons, much of this trade is between countries within the region.

- Strong growth in soybean meal imports is also projected for many other countries. Mexico's growing demand for protein feed is expected to boost imports. Russia's rising soymeal imports are linked to livestock production at larger, more modern facilities. Although China's projected growth rate for soymeal use is one of the highest in the world, most of the meal will be supplied by domestic crushing of domestically produced and imported soybeans.

Global soybean meal exports

Million metric tons

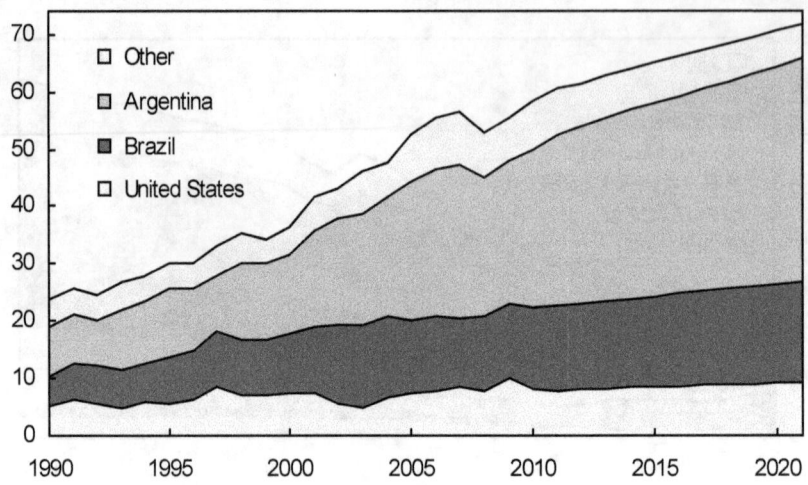

Argentina, Brazil, and the United States remain the three largest exporters of soybean meal. Together, their share of world exports rises slightly, to more than 90 percent over the next 10 years. Argentina, the world's largest soymeal exporter, increases its share of the world market from less than 49 percent in recent years to 54 percent in 2021/22.

- Argentina imposes higher export taxes on soybeans than on soybean products. This policy has provided an incentive for the country to develop a large oilseed-crushing capacity. With Argentina's low cost of soybean production and its export incentives for soybean products, soybean meal exports are projected to continue their robust growth.

- In Brazil, strong growth in domestic meal consumption due to the rapid expansion of poultry and pork production limits increases in soybean meal exports. Also, domestic soybean-crushing capacity is not expected to grow as quickly as in the past due to heavy competition from Argentina. Brazil's share of world soymeal exports remains around 25 percent.

- U.S. soybean meal exports gradually increase by about 1 million tons during the next 10 years, reaching 9.2 million tons by 2021/22. The U.S. share of world soybean meal exports declines steadily from around 15 percent in recent years to less than 13 percent by 2021/22.

- India's soybean meal exports decline as domestic use strengthens and export competition from South America intensifies. Exports fall from more than 4 million tons in most recent years, to 1.5 million by 2021, as rapidly increasing poultry, egg, and milk production absorbs more of India's domestic soybean meal production.

- The EU continues to be a small but steady exporter of soybean meal to Russia and other East European countries where livestock production is expected to increase significantly.

Global soybean oil imports

Million metric tons

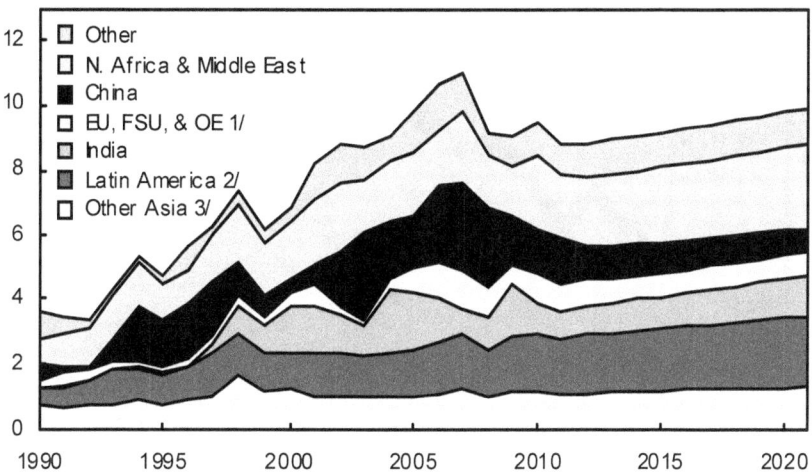

1/ European Union, former Soviet Union, and other Europe.
2/ Includes Mexico.   3/ Asia excluding India and China.

World soybean oil imports climb 1.1 million tons (12 percent) to 9.9 million tons over the 2012/13 to 2021/22 projection period, bolstered by rising food use. China and India are the countries that currently import the most soybean oil. Growth in world soybean oil trade will be constrained by competition with palm oil, which is the leading vegetable oil traded internationally.

- India is projected to replace China as the world's largest soybean oil importer. In the projections, India's soybean oil imports climb 28 percent to 1.2 million tons. Factors that contribute to the continued growth of India's soyoil imports include burgeoning demand for vegetable oils and a limited capacity to expand domestic oilseed production. Low yields, associated with excessive monsoon rainfall and low input use, also inhibit growth of oilseed production.

- In 2008, in response to high world prices, India cut its edible oil import tariffs to zero. It is assumed that during the next decade, India's soybean oil tariff will gradually return to its previous rate of 45 percent and tariffs for the other major imported oils—palm and sunflower—will remain below their historical highs of 75 to 85 percent.

- With a rapid increase in China's soybean imports for domestic crushing during the coming decade, the country's soybean oil imports are projected to decline about 50 percent to 0.7 million tons. As a result, China will no longer be the world's leading soybean oil importer.

- Income and population growth in Latin America, North Africa, and the Middle East contribute to gains in soybean oil demand and imports, although rising international prices for soybean oil will temper consumption. Nevertheless, the North Africa and Middle East region is projected to become the largest importing region, followed by Latin America.

Global soybean oil exports

Million metric tons

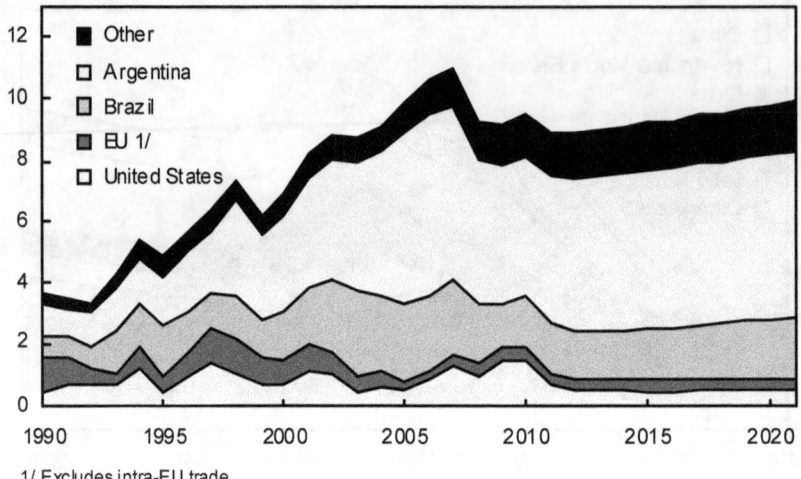

1/ Excludes intra-EU trade.

Argentina and Brazil are the world's largest soybean oil exporters, by far, and their combined share of world soybean oil exports is projected to increase slightly during the coming decade.

- Argentine soybean oil exports—the world's leading exporter—are projected to climb 8 percent to 5.4 million tons by 2021/21. Argentina's strength as a soybean oil exporter reflects the country's large crushing capacity, its small domestic market for soybean oil, and an export tax structure that favors exports of soybean products rather than soybeans. Gains in Argentine soybean production due to extensive double cropping, further adjustments in crop-pasture rotations, and the addition of marginal lands in the northwest part of the country, have also contributed to increased soybean production and crushing. Argentina's soybean oil exports declined during the last half decade due to weather-related production shortfalls and additional use of soybean oil for domestic biodiesel production. Although soyoil exports have begun to rise again and are projected to continue growing slowly, growth is restrained as more soyoil will be used for domestic biodiesel production.

- Brazil's projected increase in soybean oil exports accounts for most of the rest of the global increase in soybean oil trade. Brazil is projected to use more soybean oil for biodiesel production, but the expansion of soybean production into new areas of cultivation is expected to enable the country to increase soybean oil exports.

- U.S. soybean oil exports are projected to remain at about 0.5 million tons throughout the projection period, allowing the United States to remain the world's third-largest soybean oil exporter. U.S. soyoil exports will be constrained by increased use of soybean oil for domestic biodiesel production. Lower U.S. soybean oil exports are projected to be offset by higher exports from Argentina over the next couple of years and from Brazil in the later years of the projection period. U.S. canola oil imports from Canada and palm oil imports from Southeast Asia are projected to continue to grow strongly, and augment the U.S. edible oil supply.

- In the EU, exportable supplies of vegetable oils are limited by the growth in biodiesel production.

Global cotton imports

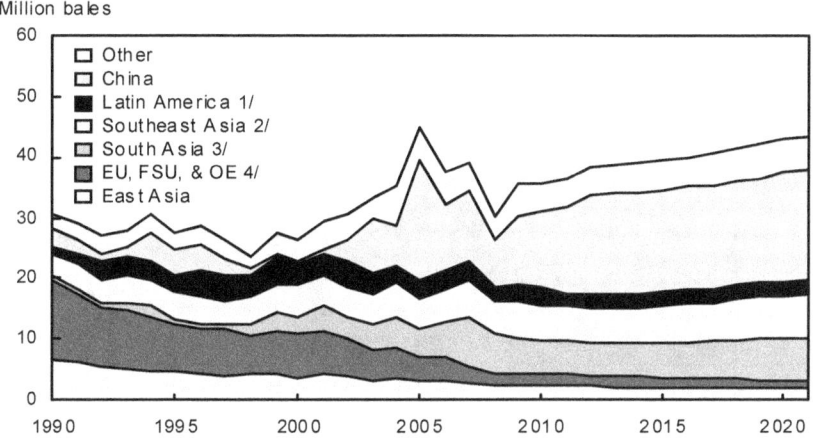

1/ Includes Mexico. 2/ Malaysia, Indonesia, Philippines, Thailand, and Vietnam. 3/ Bangladesh, India, and Pakistan. 4/ European Union, former Soviet Union, and other Europe.

World cotton trade is projected to trend upward at 1.5 percent a year until 2021, but does not surpass the 2005 record. Although geographical shifts in mill use and trade of cotton continue, they are not as dramatic as those associated with the elimination of the Multifiber Arrangement (MFA) quotas in 2005. Asia's share of world cotton imports has risen from less than 50 percent in the late 1990s to more than 77 percent in 2010 and is projected to be just above that level for the next decade.

- The textile industries in China, India, and Pakistan were the major beneficiaries of textile trade liberalization as a result of the elimination of the MFA quotas in 2005. However, imports have risen in other Asian countries as well, most notably Bangladesh and Vietnam.

- China's textile industry and cotton imports are expected to grow during the projection period, but much more slowly than the rapid increases over the past decade. Nonetheless, during the coming decade, China is projected to account for more than one-third of the global increase in cotton imports.

- In recent years, Bangladesh has become the world's second-largest cotton importer and is expected to retain that status as imports continue rising.

- Pakistan has also become a significant importer in recent years. But import growth slows in the projections as new *Bacillus thuringiensis* (*Bt*) cotton varieties specific to Pakistan's cotton growing conditions prove more productive and reduce the need for imports.

- Until several years ago, Turkey's textile industry benefited from favorable access to the EU, its major market for textile and apparel exports. However, the end of the MFA quotas gave lower cost competitors more favorable access to EU markets. Turkey's cotton imports have fallen and are projected to remain low over the next 10 years.

- The EU, Japan, Taiwan, and South Korea all reduce their cotton imports as textile trade reforms or higher wages in these economies, or both, drive textile production to countries with lower wages and other production costs.

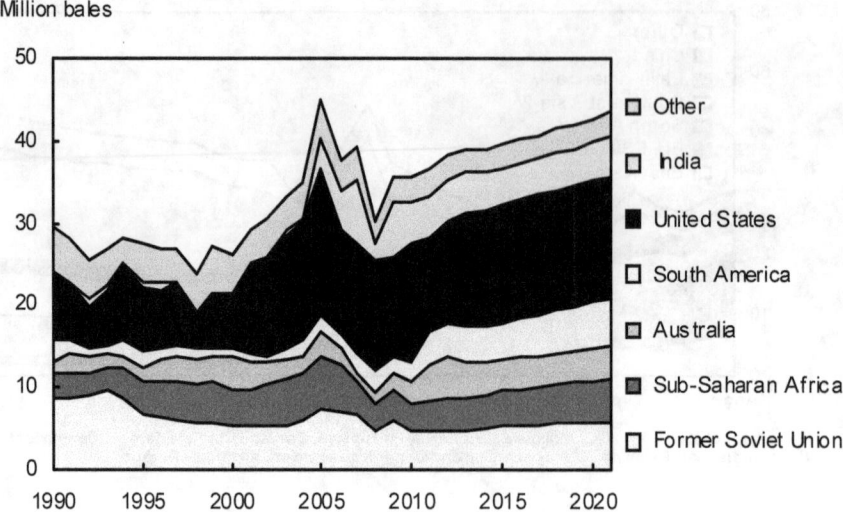

Global cotton exports

Million bales

Legend:
- Other
- India
- United States
- South America
- Australia
- Sub-Saharan Africa
- Former Soviet Union

Globalization is expected to continue to move raw cotton production to countries with favorable resource endowments and technology. Traditional producers with large land bases suitable for cotton production continue to benefit from post-MFA trade patterns, including the United States, Brazil, and Sub-Saharan Africa. The importance of technology has been highlighted by the impact of India's rapid adoption of genetically modified cotton, nearly all *Bt* cotton.

- The United States continues as the world's leading cotton exporter throughout the projections. U.S. exports rise slightly to nearly 15 million bales by 2021/22. The U.S. share of world exports rises slightly over the next several years but remains slightly below the recent historical average.

- Brazil's cotton exports are projected to increase by nearly one-third between 2012/13 and 2021/22 as the area planted to cotton expands. Exports from Brazil rise 1.3 million bales, more than from any other country or region, surpassing exports from India and Australia, and enable Brazil to become the world's second-largest cotton exporter.

- Exports from the 15 countries of the Economic Community of West African States declined sharply during the post-MFA period but are projected to rise rapidly during the coming decade due to improvements in technical and financial infrastructure, and the adoption of *Bt* cotton. The region's exports are projected to rise more than 40 percent during the next 10 years and to account for 19 percent of world trade growth. Exports from the other countries in Sub-Saharan Africa also declined after 2005 but are also projected to increase in the future, although not as robustly as from the West African Community.

- Government policies in the Central Asian countries of the FSU promoting investment in textiles have contributed to more exports of textile products rather than exports of raw cotton. However, the region's continued increase in cotton exports accounts for 17 percent of the increase in world exports.

- Improved cotton yields in India, largely due to the adoption of *Bt* cotton, have raised India's production and exports in recent years. Yield growth is projected to continue as the area planted to *Bt* cotton expands and cultivation practices improve. The increase in cotton output is expected to enable India to increase textile production and generally maintain cotton exports.

Meat exports 1/

Million metric tons

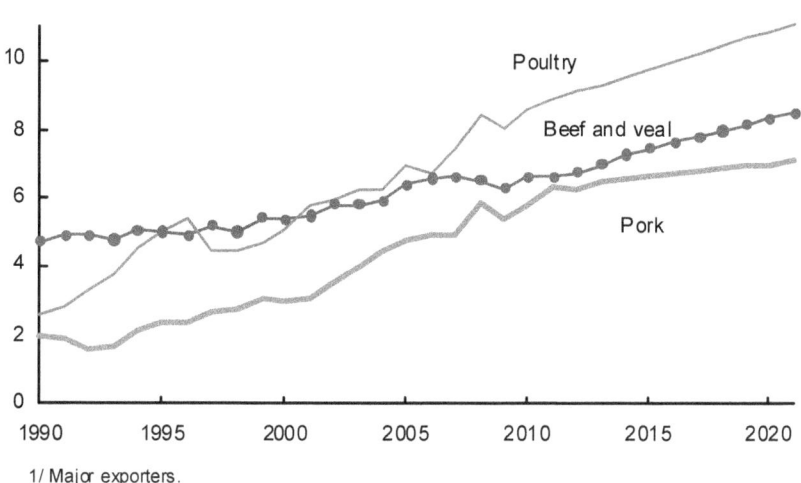

1/ Major exporters.

Growth in world meat consumption is projected to increase about 2.2 percent per year during 2012-2021. Global per capita meat consumption continues to increase and meat shipments from major exporters rise about 1.8 percent per year. The projected growth rates of exports from major exporters of beef, pork, and poultry meat are 2.5, 1.2, and 2.1 percent per year, respectively. During this period, exports rise 1.7 million tons for beef, 0.7 million for pork, and 1.9 million for poultry.

World meat trade increases 20 percent in the projections, driven primarily by rising per capita incomes and population growth in developing countries. However, Russia's meat imports decline over the coming decade, reflecting policies that stimulate meat production and curb imports.

- Beef exports from Asia, mostly from India, increased sharply after 2009. Developing countries' demand for India's lower priced beef is projected to continue rising rapidly. India's rising exports account for 40 percent of the increase in world beef trade.

- Argentine beef exports declined sharply after the 2005 peak, reflecting export restrictions on beef and changes in other policies. Argentine producers have begun to rebuild their herds and beef exports are expected to stabilize during the next several years and then rise slowly. Exports will be constrained by reduced beef imports by Russia, which has been a major market for Argentine beef.

- Exports from Brazil's expanding pork sector are expected to be competitive in price-sensitive markets such as Russia and Asian countries other than Japan and South Korea.

- During the coming decade, Brazil is expected to continue to be the largest exporter of poultry products as a result of low production costs and competitive export prices.

- Canadian beef exports and imports are each projected to rise slowly after 2012, but net exports decline somewhat in the projections. Canada's cow herd contracted significantly during 2006-10 and the rebuilding of beef herds is expected to progress slowly.

- EU beef exports are projected to decline slightly in the next 10 years.

Beef imports 1/

Million metric tons

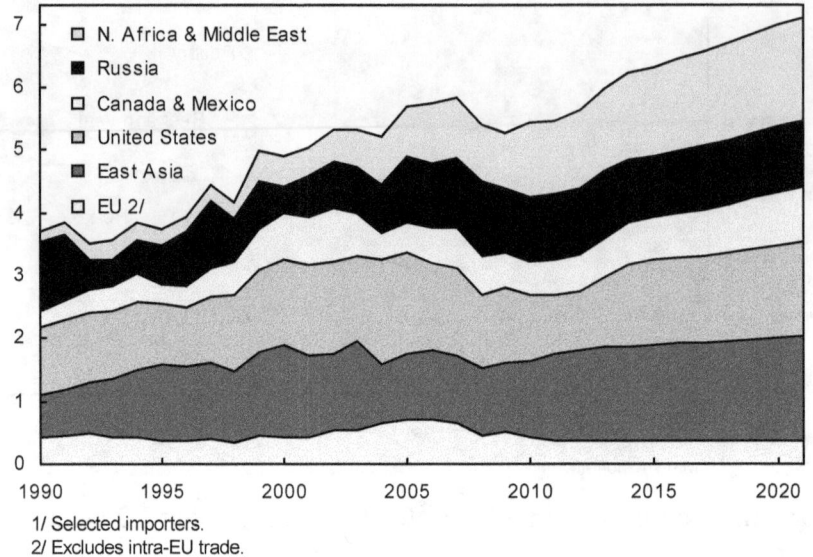

1/ Selected importers.
2/ Excludes intra-EU trade.

World beef imports declined during the 2008-09 global recession but rebounded in 2010 and 2011. Between 2012 and 2021, imports by major importers are projected to increase 25 percent and reach 8.5 million tons. Exports of lower priced beef from India and Brazil to a number of low- and middle-income countries account for much of the projected increase in world beef trade.

- During the next 10 years, Russian beef imports are projected to fluctuate around 1 million tons as rising consumer demand is offset by expanding Russian beef production and import restrictions. Russia does remain a market for EU and South American beef exports.

- Imports of grain-fed beef by higher-income countries are projected to rise steadily. U.S. beef exports to these countries are projected to increase somewhat over the next 10 years although they will have to compete with exports from other suppliers.

- U.S. beef imports, primarily of grass-fed, lean beef from Australia and New Zealand for use in ground beef and processed products, rise during the projection period. The United States replaces Russia as the world largest beef importer and accounts for 33 percent of the increase in world imports. Also, strong Asian imports of beef enable Australia and New Zealand to maintain significant levels of exports over the projection period.

- The Middle East, with a relatively fast growing population, and Asia, with high income growth rates, are projected to be growing markets for beef. Together, the two regions account for 22 percent of the increase in world beef trade through 2021.

- Strong growth in Mexican beef imports is projected to resume over the next several years. Much of Mexico's imports consist of higher valued, grain-fed beef from the United States.

Pork imports 1/

Million metric tons

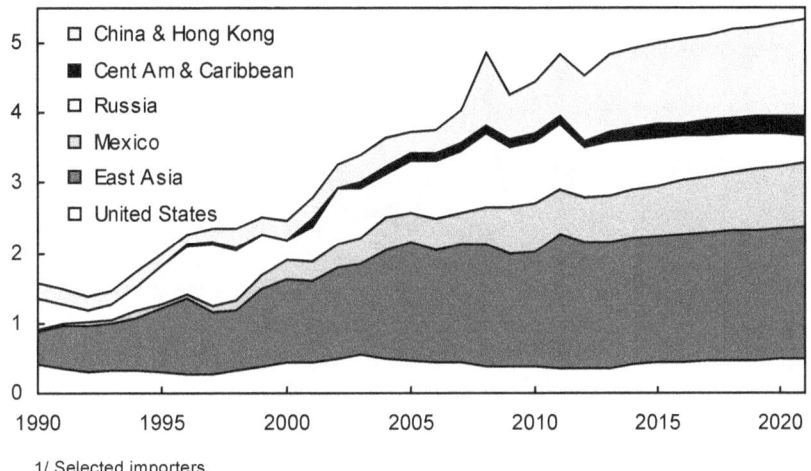

1/ Selected importers.

After the sharp 2009 drop in world pork imports that was associated with the global recession, global imports recovered in 2010.

In the projections for 2012 to 2021, world pork imports are expected to continue to rise, and to increase by 0.77 million tons (16 percent).

- Russia's pork imports are projected to decline steadily during the next 10 years in response to the country's policies to stimulate meat production and reduce imports. By 2021, Russian pork imports are projected to decline about 45 percent to less than 0.4 million tons.

- Mexican pork imports increase the most of any country in the world, rising 0.27 million tons (42 percent) between 2012 and 2021, making Mexico the world's largest growth market for pork. Increases in income and population are the primary drivers of Mexico's increasing demand for pork. Mexico accounts for 35 percent of the growth in global pork trade during the coming decade.

- Some higher income countries in East Asia increase pork imports to satisfy demand for selected cuts of pork, especially pork bellies. Japan is by far the world's largest pork importer, but as a mature market with declining population, its imports are not projected to rise significantly. Hong Kong is Asia's fastest growing pork importer and its imports account for 23 percent of the increase in world pork imports during the projection period.

- China's pork imports rose sharply in 2008 and it became a net importer. Since then, the country's pork imports have declined significantly but it remains a net importer. In the projections, pork imports rise more than exports, and the country remains a net importer through 2021.

- Imports by the Central America and Caribbean region grow more rapidly than imports by any other country or region, although from a small base. The need to import most feedstuffs limits pork production growth, while income growth and an expanding population boost demand.

Poultry imports 1/

Million metric tons

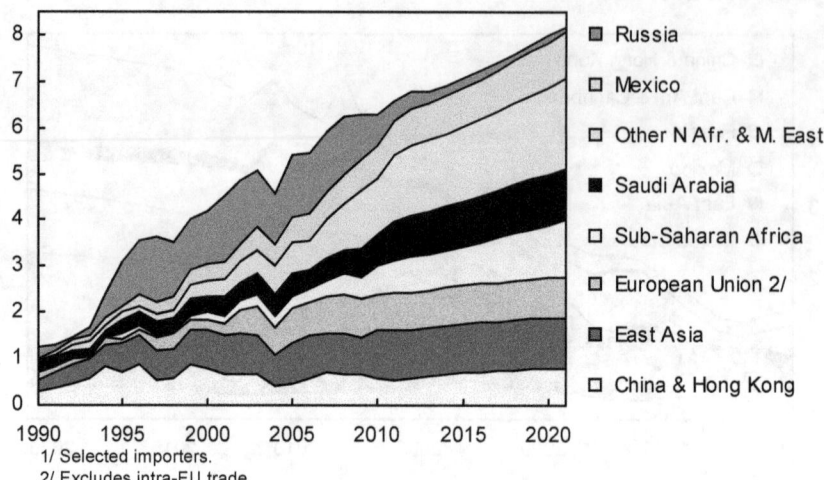

1/ Selected importers.
2/ Excludes intra-EU trade.

Poultry meat imports by major importers are projected to increase by 1.5 million tons (21 percent) between 2012 and 2021. Strong growth in imports is projected for much of the world except, most notably, for Russia and the EU (where policies limit imports), and for Japan and Canada.

- Poultry imports by Africa and the Middle East now account for more than 40 percent of imports by the major importers. Income and population growth boosts demand in the projections. In addition, ongoing animal-disease concerns in a number of countries are expected to slow growth in production and to increase demand for imports. As a result, the region's imports grow more than the rest of the world combined and by 2021 account for nearly 50 percent of world imports.

- Rising consumer incomes increase poultry demand and imports in Mexico and the Central America and Caribbean region. Poultry products remain less expensive than beef or pork, further stimulating demand. Mexico's domestic poultry production continues to increase during the projection period, but rises at a slower rate than consumption, with the result that imports rise by 0.22 million tons (28 percent).

- Russia's poultry imports are projected to decline sharply during the next 5 years. The projections assume that Russian policies will restrain poultry imports and stimulate domestic poultry production. Higher poultry prices and slower income growth inhibit per capita poultry consumption and import growth.

- In South Korea, increasing per capita consumption combined with environmental concerns that limit production growth, boost imports by 30 percent during the next decade.

- Because of avian influenza, some major poultry-exporting countries, such as Thailand and China, have shifted most of their exports to fully cooked products, and are projected to continue to do so. Because of higher production costs, these cooked products will be marketed to higher income countries in Asia, Europe, and the Middle East.

- China's rising consumption of poultry meat is met by expanding domestic production. The country's growth in poultry exports slightly exceeds the increase in imports.

Table 4. Coarse grains trade long-term projections

	2010/11	2011/12	2012/13	2013/14	2014/15	2015/16	2016/17	2017/18	2018/19	2019/20	2020/21	2021/22
	Imports, million metric tons											
Importers												
Former Soviet Union[1]	1.2	0.6	1.0	1.1	1.2	1.3	1.4	1.4	1.5	1.6	1.6	1.7
Other Europe	0.9	0.7	0.7	0.7	0.7	0.7	0.7	0.7	0.7	0.7	0.7	0.7
European Union[2]	8.4	3.7	3.4	3.5	3.7	4.2	4.2	4.2	4.2	4.1	3.9	3.6
Middle East	18.4	20.0	21.1	22.4	23.4	24.0	24.7	25.3	26.0	26.4	26.9	27.4
North Africa	12.7	12.6	14.3	14.5	14.9	15.1	15.4	15.6	15.8	15.9	16.1	16.2
Sub-Saharan Africa[3]	1.9	2.0	2.1	2.2	2.2	2.2	2.3	2.3	2.3	2.4	2.4	2.5
Japan	18.6	19.1	19.2	19.2	19.2	19.2	19.2	19.1	19.1	19.1	19.1	19.0
South Korea	8.2	8.1	9.0	9.1	9.2	9.3	9.4	9.5	9.6	9.7	9.8	9.9
Taiwan	4.5	4.6	4.6	4.5	4.5	4.5	4.5	4.5	4.5	4.6	4.6	4.6
China	2.7	4.9	6.1	7.1	8.4	9.9	11.6	13.5	15.2	17.0	18.9	21.1
Other Asia & Oceania	7.4	7.4	7.7	8.0	8.3	8.6	9.0	9.3	9.7	10.0	10.4	10.8
Mexico	10.5	12.0	13.6	14.1	15.0	15.6	16.3	17.0	17.7	18.4	19.3	20.2
Central America & Caribbean	5.0	5.2	5.3	5.4	5.5	5.6	5.7	5.8	5.9	5.9	5.9	6.0
Brazil	0.9	0.9	1.1	1.3	1.3	1.3	1.3	1.3	1.3	1.3	1.3	1.3
Other South America	9.4	9.8	9.9	10.5	10.7	10.8	10.8	11.0	11.3	11.4	11.5	11.6
Other foreign[4]	1.9	4.8	5.1	5.1	5.3	5.3	5.3	5.2	5.1	5.1	5.0	4.9
United States	2.9	2.6	2.7	2.7	2.7	2.7	2.7	2.7	2.7	2.7	2.7	2.7
Total trade	115.3	118.9	127.1	131.3	136.1	140.4	144.3	148.4	152.5	156.2	160.0	164.0
	Exports, million metric tons											
Exporters												
European Union[2]	6.1	4.8	5.2	5.4	5.6	5.9	6.1	6.3	6.5	6.8	7.0	7.3
China	0.2	0.3	0.2	0.3	0.3	0.3	0.3	0.2	0.2	0.2	0.2	0.2
Argentina	18.5	24.3	24.7	25.0	25.3	25.4	25.8	26.2	26.8	27.3	28.0	28.7
Australia	5.4	5.0	4.9	5.0	5.0	5.2	5.3	5.3	5.4	5.4	5.5	5.6
Canada	4.5	2.8	4.1	4.0	4.0	4.0	4.0	3.9	3.9	3.9	3.9	3.8
South Africa	3.0	2.0	2.0	2.2	2.2	2.1	2.2	2.2	2.2	2.2	2.1	2.1
Other Europe	2.2	2.1	2.2	2.3	2.4	2.5	2.7	2.9	3.0	3.2	3.4	3.6
Former Soviet Union[1]	8.8	19.1	16.6	17.6	18.6	19.5	20.4	21.3	22.0	23.0	23.9	25.0
Other foreign	16.0	15.3	15.5	15.3	14.8	14.9	16.0	16.9	18.2	19.2	20.4	21.4
United States	50.7	43.2	51.8	54.1	57.9	60.5	61.7	63.0	64.3	64.9	65.5	66.2
	Percent											
U.S. trade share	44.0	36.3	40.8	41.2	42.6	43.1	42.8	42.5	42.2	41.6	41.0	40.4

1/ Covers FSU-12, includes intra-FSU trade.
2/ Covers EU-27, excludes intra-EU trade.
3/ Includes South Africa.
4/ Includes unaccounted.
The projections were completed in November 2011.

Table 5. Corn trade long-term projections

	2010/11	2011/12	2012/13	2013/14	2014/15	2015/16	2016/17	2017/18	2018/19	2019/20	2020/21	2021/22
						Imports, million metric tons						
Importers												
European Union[1]	7.3	3.5	3.2	3.3	3.5	4.0	4.0	4.0	4.0	3.9	3.6	3.3
Former Soviet Union[2]	0.3	0.2	0.5	0.5	0.6	0.6	0.7	0.7	0.7	0.7	0.8	0.8
Egypt	5.4	6.0	6.8	6.8	7.0	7.0	7.1	7.2	7.2	7.3	7.3	7.3
Morocco	1.8	1.9	2.1	2.2	2.4	2.4	2.5	2.6	2.6	2.7	2.8	2.8
Other North Africa	4.1	4.0	4.2	4.2	4.2	4.2	4.3	4.3	4.3	4.3	4.3	4.3
Iran	3.5	3.5	3.6	4.0	4.3	4.6	4.8	5.0	5.2	5.3	5.4	5.5
Saudi Arabia	1.9	2.0	2.2	2.3	2.5	2.5	2.7	2.7	2.9	2.9	3.1	3.2
Turkey	0.5	0.5	0.6	0.7	0.9	0.9	1.0	1.1	1.1	1.2	1.3	1.3
Other Middle East	4.0	4.4	4.5	4.5	4.6	4.7	4.8	4.8	4.9	4.9	5.0	5.0
Japan	15.7	16.1	16.2	16.1	16.1	16.1	16.1	16.1	16.1	16.0	16.0	16.0
South Korea	8.1	8.0	8.9	9.0	9.1	9.3	9.3	9.5	9.6	9.7	9.7	9.8
Taiwan	4.3	4.4	4.5	4.4	4.4	4.4	4.4	4.4	4.4	4.4	4.4	4.4
China	1.0	3.0	4.0	4.9	6.1	7.5	9.0	10.8	12.5	14.2	16.0	18.1
Indonesia	2.5	1.5	1.5	1.5	1.6	1.6	1.7	1.8	1.9	1.9	2.0	2.1
Malaysia	2.7	3.3	3.4	3.5	3.6	3.6	3.7	3.7	3.8	3.8	3.9	3.9
Other Asia & Oceania	2.1	2.5	2.8	3.0	3.1	3.3	3.5	3.7	4.0	4.2	4.4	4.7
Canada	0.9	1.4	1.4	1.5	1.6	1.7	1.6	1.6	1.5	1.4	1.4	1.3
Mexico	8.0	9.8	10.8	10.9	11.5	11.9	12.5	13.0	13.6	14.2	15.0	15.7
Central America & Caribbean	5.0	5.2	5.3	5.4	5.5	5.6	5.7	5.8	5.8	5.9	5.9	6.0
Brazil	0.5	0.5	0.7	0.8	0.8	0.8	0.8	0.8	0.8	0.8	0.8	0.8
Other South America	7.9	8.2	8.4	8.9	9.0	9.1	9.1	9.3	9.5	9.6	9.7	9.8
Sub-Saharan Africa[3]	1.2	1.4	1.4	1.4	1.5	1.5	1.5	1.6	1.6	1.6	1.7	1.7
Other foreign[4]	1.0	3.6	3.1	3.1	3.1	3.1	3.1	3.1	3.1	3.1	3.1	3.1
United States	0.7	0.4	0.4	0.4	0.4	0.4	0.4	0.4	0.4	0.4	0.4	0.4
Total trade	90.5	95.1	100.4	103.2	107.2	111.0	114.2	117.8	121.3	124.5	127.8	131.3
						Exports, million metric tons						
Exporters												
European Union[1]	1.0	2.0	2.1	2.2	2.2	2.4	2.4	2.5	2.5	2.6	2.6	2.7
China	0.1	0.2	0.2	0.2	0.2	0.2	0.2	0.1	0.1	0.1	0.1	0.1
Argentina	15.0	20.0	20.1	20.2	20.0	20.0	20.1	20.5	20.8	21.3	21.9	22.6
Brazil	9.0	8.5	8.7	8.5	8.0	8.0	8.9	9.7	10.8	11.8	12.8	13.7
South Africa	3.0	2.0	2.0	2.2	2.2	2.1	2.1	2.2	2.2	2.1	2.1	2.1
Other Europe	2.2	2.1	2.2	2.2	2.4	2.5	2.7	2.9	3.0	3.2	3.4	3.5
Former Soviet Union[2]	5.2	12.9	10.9	11.5	12.2	13.0	13.6	14.4	14.8	15.6	16.4	17.4
Other foreign	8.4	6.8	6.6	6.7	6.7	6.9	7.0	7.2	7.3	7.4	7.5	7.6
United States	46.6	40.6	47.6	49.5	53.3	55.9	57.2	58.4	59.7	60.3	61.0	61.6
						Percent						
U.S. trade share	51.5	42.7	47.5	48.0	49.7	50.4	50.0	49.6	49.2	48.5	47.7	46.9

1/ Covers EU-27, excludes intra-EU trade.
2/ Covers FSU-12, includes intra-FSU trade.
3/ Includes South Africa.
4/ Includes unaccounted.
The projections were completed in November 2011.

Table 6. Barley trade long-term projections

	2010/11	2011/12	2012/13	2013/14	2014/15	2015/16	2016/17	2017/18	2018/19	2019/20	2020/21	2021/22
					Imports, million metric tons							
Importers												
Former Soviet Union[1]	0.7	0.4	0.5	0.5	0.6	0.6	0.7	0.7	0.7	0.8	0.8	0.8
Japan	1.4	1.3	1.3	1.3	1.3	1.3	1.3	1.3	1.3	1.3	1.3	1.3
China	1.7	1.8	1.9	2.1	2.2	2.3	2.4	2.5	2.6	2.6	2.7	2.8
Latin America[2]	0.9	0.8	0.8	0.8	0.9	0.9	0.9	1.0	1.0	1.0	1.1	1.1
Saudi Arabia	6.2	7.2	7.3	7.6	7.6	7.7	7.8	7.8	7.9	8.0	8.1	8.1
Iran	0.4	0.4	0.8	0.9	1.0	1.0	1.1	1.1	1.2	1.3	1.3	1.4
Other Middle East	1.6	1.7	1.9	2.0	2.1	2.1	2.2	2.2	2.3	2.3	2.4	2.4
Morocco	0.2	0.2	0.2	0.2	0.3	0.3	0.3	0.4	0.4	0.4	0.5	0.5
Other North Africa	1.0	0.8	0.8	0.9	0.9	0.9	0.9	1.0	1.0	1.0	1.1	1.1
Other foreign[3]	1.0	0.8	1.0	1.1	1.1	1.1	1.1	1.1	1.1	1.2	1.2	1.2
United States	0.5	0.5	0.4	0.4	0.4	0.4	0.4	0.4	0.4	0.4	0.4	0.4
Total trade	15.6	15.9	17.0	17.9	18.3	18.7	19.2	19.6	20.0	20.5	20.8	21.2
					Exports, million metric tons							
Exporters												
European Union[4]	4.9	2.5	2.8	2.9	3.0	3.1	3.2	3.4	3.5	3.8	3.9	4.2
Australia	4.2	4.0	4.0	4.2	4.3	4.4	4.5	4.6	4.6	4.7	4.8	4.8
Canada	1.2	0.7	1.8	1.8	1.7	1.7	1.7	1.6	1.6	1.6	1.6	1.5
Russia	0.3	1.8	1.0	1.0	1.0	1.0	1.0	1.0	1.0	1.0	1.0	1.0
Ukraine	2.8	4.1	4.1	4.5	4.6	4.6	4.8	4.9	5.0	5.0	5.1	5.1
Other Former Soviet Union[5]	0.3	0.3	0.4	0.5	0.6	0.7	0.8	0.9	1.0	1.1	1.2	1.3
Turkey	0.1	0.2	0.3	0.3	0.3	0.3	0.3	0.3	0.3	0.3	0.3	0.3
Other foreign	1.7	2.2	2.4	2.5	2.5	2.6	2.6	2.7	2.7	2.7	2.8	2.8
United States	0.2	0.2	0.2	0.2	0.2	0.2	0.2	0.2	0.2	0.2	0.2	0.2
					Percent							
U.S. trade share	1.4	1.4	1.3	1.2	1.2	1.2	1.1	1.1	1.1	1.1	1.0	1.0

1/ Covers FSU-12, includes intra-FSU trade.
2/ Includes Mexico.
3/ Includes unaccounted.
4/ Covers EU-27, excludes intra-EU trade.
5/ Covers FSU-12 except Russia and Ukraine, includes intra-FSU trade.
The projections were completed in November 2011.

Table 7. Sorghum trade long-term projections

	2010/11	2011/12	2012/13	2013/14	2014/15	2015/16	2016/17	2017/18	2018/19	2019/20	2020/21	2021/22
Importers						*Imports, million metric tons*						
Japan	1.4	1.6	1.6	1.6	1.6	1.6	1.6	1.6	1.6	1.6	1.6	1.6
Mexico	2.4	2.1	2.8	3.1	3.4	3.5	3.7	3.8	3.9	4.0	4.1	4.2
North Africa & Middle East	0.2	0.2	0.2	0.2	0.2	0.2	0.2	0.2	0.2	0.2	0.2	0.2
South America	1.0	1.2	1.2	1.3	1.3	1.3	1.3	1.3	1.3	1.3	1.2	1.2
Sub-Saharan Africa[1]	0.5	0.5	0.6	0.6	0.6	0.6	0.6	0.6	0.7	0.7	0.7	0.7
Other[2]	1.4	0.0	0.8	0.8	0.8	0.8	0.8	0.8	0.8	0.8	0.8	0.8
Total trade	7.0	5.5	7.2	7.7	8.0	8.1	8.3	8.3	8.5	8.6	8.7	8.8
Exporters						*Exports, million metric tons*						
Argentina	1.9	2.2	2.3	2.5	2.8	2.9	3.1	3.2	3.3	3.3	3.4	3.5
Australia	1.0	0.8	0.7	0.6	0.6	0.6	0.6	0.6	0.6	0.6	0.6	0.6
Other foreign	0.3	0.3	0.3	0.3	0.3	0.3	0.3	0.3	0.3	0.3	0.3	0.3
United States	3.8	2.3	3.9	4.3	4.3	4.3	4.3	4.3	4.3	4.3	4.3	4.3
						Percent						
U.S. trade share	54.7	41.3	54.6	56.4	54.1	53.2	52.2	51.8	50.8	50.4	49.8	49.2

1/ Includes South Africa.
2/ EU-27 and the rest of the world. Excludes intra-EU trade. Includes unaccounted.
The projections were completed in November 2011.

Table 8. Wheat trade long-term projections

	2010/11	2011/12	2012/13	2013/14	2014/15	2015/16	2016/17	2017/18	2018/19	2019/20	2020/21	2021/22
	Imports, million metric tons											
Importers												
Morocco	3.9	3.0	3.7	3.7	3.7	3.8	3.8	3.9	3.9	3.9	4.0	4.1
Egypt	10.6	10.5	10.7	10.9	11.1	11.3	11.5	11.7	11.9	12.1	12.3	12.5
Other North Africa	9.6	9.5	9.4	9.1	8.8	8.5	8.3	8.3	8.4	8.5	8.6	8.7
Saudi Arabia	1.7	2.0	2.1	2.3	2.4	2.5	2.7	2.8	2.9	3.0	3.1	3.2
Iran	0.5	0.2	0.2	0.2	0.2	0.2	0.2	0.2	0.2	0.2	0.2	0.2
Iraq	3.6	3.7	3.9	4.1	4.1	4.2	4.4	4.5	4.6	4.7	4.9	5.0
Other Middle East	7.9	9.1	9.5	9.7	9.9	10.1	10.3	10.5	10.6	10.8	11.0	11.1
West African Community[1]	6.0	5.9	6.3	6.4	6.4	6.6	6.9	7.1	7.4	7.6	7.9	8.2
Other Sub-Saharan Africa[2]	8.4	9.5	9.6	9.8	10.0	10.3	10.6	10.8	11.1	11.4	11.7	11.9
Mexico	3.5	3.5	3.5	3.5	3.6	3.7	3.7	3.8	3.8	3.9	3.9	4.0
Central America & Caribbean	3.6	3.6	3.7	3.7	3.7	3.7	3.7	3.8	3.8	3.8	3.8	3.8
Brazil	6.7	7.0	7.0	7.1	7.3	7.4	7.4	7.5	7.6	7.6	7.7	7.8
Other South America	6.2	6.3	6.5	6.5	6.6	6.7	6.7	6.8	6.8	6.9	6.9	6.9
European Union[3]	4.7	7.5	5.3	5.9	6.2	6.3	6.4	6.6	6.5	6.5	6.4	6.3
Other Europe	1.6	1.7	2.1	1.9	1.8	1.8	1.8	1.9	1.9	1.9	2.0	2.0
Former Soviet Union[4]	5.5	6.2	6.0	6.1	6.3	6.4	6.4	6.5	6.5	6.6	6.6	6.7
Japan	5.9	5.8	5.7	5.7	5.7	5.7	5.7	5.7	5.7	5.7	5.7	5.7
South Korea	4.8	4.2	4.4	4.3	4.3	4.3	4.2	4.2	4.2	4.1	4.1	4.1
Philippines	3.2	3.0	3.1	3.1	3.2	3.2	3.3	3.3	3.4	3.5	3.5	3.6
Indonesia	6.6	6.7	6.8	6.9	7.1	7.2	7.4	7.5	7.6	7.8	8.0	8.2
China	0.9	1.5	1.5	1.3	1.4	1.4	1.5	1.6	1.6	1.7	1.8	1.8
Bangladesh	3.9	2.8	3.3	3.4	3.5	3.6	3.7	3.8	3.9	4.0	4.1	4.2
Malaysia	1.5	1.4	1.4	1.4	1.4	1.4	1.5	1.5	1.5	1.5	1.5	1.5
Thailand	1.9	1.6	1.5	1.6	1.6	1.7	1.7	1.7	1.8	1.8	1.8	1.9
Vietnam	2.5	2.2	1.9	1.9	2.0	2.0	2.1	2.1	2.2	2.2	2.3	2.4
Pakistan	0.2	0.2	0.1	0.0	0.1	0.1	0.1	0.1	0.1	0.1	0.1	0.1
Other Asia & Oceania	7.5	7.9	8.3	8.5	8.7	8.9	9.2	9.6	9.9	10.2	10.5	10.9
Other foreign[5]	5.6	7.4	6.5	6.1	6.3	6.3	6.4	6.4	6.4	6.5	6.5	6.5
United States	2.6	3.3	3.0	3.0	3.1	3.1	3.3	3.3	3.4	3.4	3.5	3.5
Total trade	131.4	137.3	136.8	138.2	140.5	142.4	144.8	147.1	149.5	151.8	154.3	156.9
	Exports, million metric tons											
Exporters												
European Union[3]	22.9	17.0	17.0	19.7	20.3	20.8	22.1	22.8	23.2	23.6	24.9	25.9
Canada	16.5	18.0	17.0	17.1	17.1	17.2	17.2	17.3	17.4	17.4	17.5	17.5
Australia	18.3	19.0	19.3	18.7	18.9	19.0	19.1	19.2	19.4	19.5	19.7	19.8
Argentina	9.3	7.5	8.2	8.3	8.4	8.7	8.9	9.1	9.4	9.6	9.8	10.0
Russia	4.0	19.0	18.8	17.5	19.5	20.0	20.7	21.1	21.8	22.7	23.5	23.8
Ukraine	4.3	8.0	8.0	8.3	8.5	8.9	9.3	9.7	10.2	10.7	11.2	11.6
Other Former Soviet Union[6]	5.8	8.7	8.3	8.1	8.2	8.6	9.0	9.2	9.4	9.6	9.9	10.4
Other Europe	0.8	0.6	0.6	0.6	0.6	0.7	0.7	0.7	0.7	0.7	0.7	0.7
India	0.1	1.0	1.5	2.0	1.0	0.9	0.8	0.7	0.6	0.6	0.5	0.5
China	0.9	1.0	1.1	1.1	1.2	1.3	1.3	1.4	1.4	1.4	1.5	1.5
Turkey	3.0	3.5	3.2	3.0	3.0	3.1	3.0	3.1	3.0	3.0	3.0	3.0
Other foreign	10.4	7.5	7.9	7.9	7.8	7.7	7.6	7.7	7.7	7.8	7.8	7.8
United States	35.1	26.5	25.8	25.8	25.9	25.9	25.2	25.2	25.2	25.2	24.5	24.5
	Percent											
U.S. trade share	26.7	19.3	18.9	18.7	18.4	18.2	17.4	17.1	16.8	16.6	15.9	15.6

1/ Economic Community of West African States
2/ Includes South Africa.
3/ Covers EU-27, excludes intra-EU trade.
4/ Covers FSU-12, includes intra-FSU trade.
5/ Includes unaccounted.
6/ Covers FSU-12 except Russia and Ukraine, includes intra-FSU trade.
The projections were completed in November 2011.

Table 9. Rice trade long-term projections

	2010/11	2011/12	2012/13	2013/14	2014/15	2015/16	2016/17	2017/18	2018/19	2019/20	2020/21	2021/22
	Imports, million metric tons											
Importers												
Canada	0.34	0.35	0.36	0.36	0.37	0.37	0.38	0.39	0.39	0.40	0.40	0.41
Mexico	0.66	0.73	0.77	0.80	0.83	0.86	0.89	0.91	0.94	0.97	0.99	1.02
Central America/Caribbean	1.56	1.46	1.67	1.73	1.75	1.78	1.82	1.86	1.89	1.93	1.97	2.01
Brazil	0.60	0.50	0.58	0.58	0.59	0.59	0.59	0.60	0.60	0.61	0.61	0.61
Other South America	0.68	0.77	0.72	0.73	0.72	0.70	0.72	0.73	0.75	0.75	0.76	0.76
European Union[1]	1.15	1.17	1.30	1.34	1.37	1.39	1.41	1.43	1.45	1.47	1.49	1.51
Former Soviet Union[2]	0.38	0.36	0.36	0.39	0.39	0.38	0.38	0.39	0.39	0.38	0.38	0.37
Other Europe	0.14	0.14	0.15	0.15	0.15	0.15	0.15	0.15	0.15	0.15	0.15	0.15
Bangladesh	1.56	0.80	0.82	0.89	0.95	1.02	1.08	1.14	1.20	1.26	1.31	1.35
China	0.54	0.48	0.53	0.50	0.51	0.50	0.53	0.56	0.59	0.61	0.63	0.65
Japan	0.70	0.70	0.68	0.68	0.68	0.68	0.68	0.68	0.68	0.68	0.68	0.68
South Korea	0.33	0.35	0.39	0.41	0.41	0.41	0.41	0.41	0.41	0.41	0.41	0.41
Indonesia	2.20	1.40	1.90	1.87	2.11	2.34	2.51	2.67	2.86	3.01	3.16	3.30
Malaysia	1.04	1.13	1.17	1.25	1.31	1.36	1.40	1.44	1.47	1.50	1.52	1.54
Philippines	1.50	2.20	2.42	2.61	2.71	2.80	2.89	3.01	3.12	3.25	3.36	3.46
Other Asia & Oceania	2.44	2.25	2.42	2.57	2.69	2.75	2.80	2.85	2.91	2.96	3.01	3.07
Iraq	1.15	1.20	1.25	1.28	1.31	1.34	1.36	1.39	1.41	1.43	1.45	1.47
Iran	1.30	1.50	1.56	1.54	1.53	1.53	1.51	1.49	1.48	1.46	1.44	1.42
Saudi Arabia	1.10	1.15	1.12	1.13	1.15	1.17	1.19	1.22	1.24	1.27	1.29	1.32
Other N. Africa & M. East	2.39	2.40	2.43	2.50	2.58	2.64	2.69	2.74	2.79	2.84	2.90	2.95
West African Community[3]	6.45	6.26	6.97	7.42	7.84	8.32	8.75	9.10	9.38	9.64	9.88	10.13
Other Sub-Saharan Africa[4]	2.12	2.25	2.29	2.39	2.49	2.59	2.69	2.79	2.89	2.98	3.08	3.19
South Africa	0.76	0.80	0.83	0.84	0.85	0.87	0.88	0.90	0.92	0.93	0.95	0.96
Other foreign[5]	2.04	1.96	1.54	1.54	1.54	1.54	1.54	1.54	1.54	1.54	1.54	1.54
United States	0.58	0.60	0.62	0.64	0.66	0.67	0.69	0.71	0.73	0.75	0.77	0.79
Total imports	33.68	32.88	34.84	36.15	37.49	38.75	39.95	41.09	42.16	43.17	44.13	45.07
	Exports, million metric tons											
Exporters												
Australia	0.35	0.45	0.45	0.46	0.46	0.46	0.46	0.47	0.47	0.47	0.47	0.48
Argentina	0.65	0.65	0.67	0.68	0.70	0.72	0.75	0.77	0.79	0.81	0.84	0.86
Other South America	2.64	2.29	2.16	2.25	2.28	2.36	2.44	2.52	2.59	2.67	2.76	2.85
European Union[1]	0.25	0.35	0.34	0.35	0.36	0.36	0.37	0.38	0.39	0.39	0.40	0.41
China	0.50	0.60	0.63	0.73	0.84	0.94	0.99	1.06	1.10	1.14	1.18	1.21
India	2.80	4.50	4.01	4.26	4.49	4.57	4.74	4.87	4.93	4.95	4.86	4.71
Pakistan	2.80	3.75	3.86	3.92	4.04	4.03	4.06	4.11	4.20	4.31	4.41	4.52
Thailand	10.50	8.00	9.90	10.19	10.76	11.36	11.87	12.34	12.74	13.11	13.55	13.99
Vietnam	7.00	6.70	6.50	6.70	6.91	7.12	7.31	7.47	7.67	7.82	7.99	8.15
Burma	0.90	0.75	0.90	0.88	0.80	0.82	0.84	0.87	0.90	0.91	0.92	0.92
Cambodia	1.00	0.80	0.90	1.04	1.07	1.12	1.16	1.21	1.27	1.35	1.43	1.52
Egypt	0.08	0.50	0.64	0.62	0.61	0.56	0.52	0.51	0.52	0.53	0.55	0.57
Other foreign	0.73	0.62	0.61	0.60	0.61	0.61	0.63	0.65	0.68	0.71	0.73	0.76
United States	3.49	2.92	3.26	3.46	3.57	3.71	3.81	3.85	3.93	4.00	4.04	4.12
Total exports	33.68	32.88	34.84	36.15	37.49	38.75	39.95	41.09	42.16	43.17	44.13	45.07
	Percent											
U.S. trade share	10.4	8.9	9.4	9.6	9.5	9.6	9.5	9.4	9.3	9.3	9.2	9.1

1/ Covers EU-27, excludes intra-EU trade.
2/ Covers FSU-12, includes intra-FSU trade.
3/ Economic Community of West African States.
4/ Excludes South Africa.
5/ Includes unaccounted.
The projections were completed in November 2011.

Table 10. Soybean trade long-term projections

	2010/11	2011/12	2012/13	2013/14	2014/15	2015/16	2016/17	2017/18	2018/19	2019/20	2020/21	2021/22
	Imports, million metric tons											
Importers												
European Union[1]	12.9	12.6	12.9	12.4	12.3	12.1	12.0	11.9	11.8	11.7	11.6	11.5
Japan	2.9	3.0	3.0	2.8	2.8	2.7	2.7	2.7	2.7	2.6	2.6	2.6
South Korea	1.2	1.3	1.3	1.3	1.3	1.3	1.3	1.3	1.3	1.3	1.3	1.3
Taiwan	2.4	2.6	2.6	2.6	2.6	2.7	2.7	2.7	2.7	2.6	2.6	2.6
Mexico	3.5	3.5	3.5	3.6	3.7	3.8	3.9	4.0	4.0	4.1	4.2	4.3
Former Soviet Union[2]	1.0	1.1	1.1	1.1	1.1	1.1	1.1	1.1	1.1	1.1	1.1	1.2
Other Europe	4.7	5.3	5.5	5.7	5.8	6.0	6.1	6.3	6.4	6.6	6.7	6.9
China	52.3	56.5	63.1	66.1	69.0	72.0	75.0	78.0	81.0	84.0	87.0	90.0
Malaysia	0.6	0.6	0.6	0.7	0.7	0.7	0.7	0.7	0.7	0.7	0.7	0.8
Indonesia	1.7	1.7	1.8	1.8	1.8	1.9	1.9	1.9	2.0	2.0	2.0	2.1
Other	9.1	8.7	9.8	9.9	10.7	11.5	12.2	12.4	12.7	13.6	13.8	14.3
Total imports	92.4	96.9	105.1	107.9	111.9	115.8	119.6	123.0	126.4	130.5	133.8	137.4
	Exports, million metric tons											
Exporters												
Argentina	9.2	10.8	12.2	12.2	12.2	13.0	13.6	14.2	15.0	15.7	16.3	16.9
Brazil	30.0	38.0	41.3	41.3	44.1	46.2	48.6	50.7	52.6	55.1	56.9	59.2
Other South America	8.0	7.6	8.1	8.5	8.9	9.3	9.8	10.2	10.6	11.1	11.6	12.0
Ukraine	1.0	1.4	1.5	1.4	1.5	1.5	1.6	1.7	1.8	1.8	2.0	2.0
Other foreign	3.4	3.1	3.1	3.3	3.4	3.5	3.5	3.6	3.7	3.7	3.8	3.9
United States	40.9	36.1	38.9	41.2	41.8	42.3	42.5	42.6	42.7	43.0	43.3	43.4
Total exports	92.4	96.9	105.1	107.9	111.9	115.8	119.6	123.0	126.4	130.5	133.8	137.4
	Percent											
U.S. trade share	44.2	37.2	37.0	38.2	37.3	36.5	35.5	34.6	33.8	33.0	32.3	31.6

1/ Covers EU-27, excludes intra-EU trade.
2/ Covers FSU-12, includes intra-FSU trade.
The projections were completed in November 2011.

Table 11. Soybean meal trade long-term projections

	2010/11	2011/12	2012/13	2013/14	2014/15	2015/16	2016/17	2017/18	2018/19	2019/20	2020/21	2021/22
					Imports, million metric tons							
Importers												
European Union[1]	22.0	23.0	23.0	23.2	23.4	23.5	23.7	23.9	24.1	24.3	24.5	24.6
Former Soviet Union[2]	0.8	0.6	0.5	0.6	0.6	0.7	0.7	0.7	0.7	0.8	0.8	0.8
Other Europe	0.6	0.6	0.6	0.6	0.7	0.7	0.7	0.7	0.7	0.7	0.7	0.7
Canada	1.1	1.1	1.1	1.1	1.1	1.1	1.2	1.2	1.2	1.2	1.3	1.3
Japan	2.2	2.3	2.4	2.4	2.4	2.5	2.5	2.5	2.5	2.5	2.6	2.6
Southeast Asia	10.6	10.7	11.0	11.4	11.8	12.1	12.4	12.8	13.2	13.6	14.0	14.4
Mexico	1.5	1.5	1.6	1.6	1.7	1.7	1.7	1.8	1.8	1.9	1.9	2.0
Other Latin America	6.2	6.4	6.6	6.8	7.1	7.3	7.5	7.7	8.0	8.2	8.4	8.6
North Africa & Middle East	6.3	6.5	6.6	6.8	6.9	7.1	7.2	7.4	7.5	7.7	7.9	8.1
Other	7.1	8.0	8.2	8.3	8.4	8.4	8.5	8.6	8.6	8.7	8.7	8.9
Total imports	58.3	60.6	61.5	62.9	64.0	65.0	66.1	67.2	68.3	69.5	70.6	71.9
					Exports, million metric tons							
Exporters												
Argentina	27.5	29.8	30.6	32.0	32.9	33.6	34.5	35.3	36.1	37.0	37.9	39.0
Brazil	14.0	14.8	15.1	15.1	15.4	15.7	16.0	16.3	16.7	17.0	17.3	17.7
Other South America	2.2	2.2	2.2	2.3	2.3	2.4	2.4	2.5	2.5	2.6	2.6	2.6
China	0.5	0.7	0.7	0.7	0.7	0.8	0.8	0.8	0.8	0.8	0.8	0.8
India	4.6	4.2	3.7	3.4	3.2	2.9	2.7	2.4	2.2	2.0	1.7	1.5
European Union[1]	0.6	0.5	0.5	0.5	0.5	0.5	0.5	0.5	0.5	0.5	0.5	0.5
Other foreign	0.6	0.6	0.6	0.6	0.6	0.6	0.6	0.6	0.6	0.6	0.6	0.7
United States	8.3	8.0	8.1	8.3	8.5	8.6	8.7	8.8	8.9	9.0	9.1	9.2
Total exports	58.3	60.6	61.5	62.9	64.0	65.0	66.1	67.2	68.3	69.5	70.6	71.9
					Percent							
U.S. trade share	14.2	13.2	13.2	13.3	13.3	13.3	13.2	13.1	13.1	13.0	12.9	12.8

1/ Covers EU-27, excludes intra-EU trade.
2/ Covers FSU-12, includes intra-FSU trade.
The projections were completed in November 2011.

Table 12. Soybean oil trade long-term projections

	2010/11	2011/12	2012/13	2013/14	2014/15	2015/16	2016/17	2017/18	2018/19	2019/20	2020/21	2021/22
					Imports, million metric tons							
Importers												
China	1.3	1.4	1.0	1.0	1.0	1.0	0.9	0.9	0.8	0.8	0.7	0.7
India	0.9	0.9	0.9	0.9	1.0	1.0	1.0	1.1	1.1	1.1	1.2	1.2
Other Asia	1.2	1.1	1.1	1.1	1.2	1.2	1.2	1.2	1.3	1.3	1.3	1.4
Latin America	1.7	1.7	1.8	1.8	1.9	1.9	2.0	2.0	2.1	2.1	2.1	2.2
North Africa & Middle East	2.3	2.0	2.2	2.2	2.3	2.3	2.4	2.4	2.4	2.5	2.6	2.6
European Union[1]	0.9	0.8	0.7	0.7	0.7	0.7	0.7	0.7	0.7	0.7	0.7	0.7
Other	1.1	1.0	1.1	1.1	1.1	1.1	1.2	1.2	1.2	1.2	1.2	1.2
Total imports	9.5	8.9	8.9	8.9	9.0	9.2	9.3	9.4	9.6	9.7	9.8	9.9
					Exports, million metric tons							
Exporters												
Argentina	4.5	4.8	5.0	5.1	5.2	5.2	5.2	5.3	5.3	5.3	5.4	5.4
Brazil	1.7	1.7	1.5	1.5	1.6	1.7	1.7	1.8	1.8	1.9	1.9	2.0
European Union[1]	0.4	0.4	0.4	0.4	0.4	0.4	0.4	0.4	0.4	0.4	0.4	0.3
Other foreign	1.4	1.3	1.4	1.4	1.5	1.5	1.5	1.5	1.6	1.6	1.6	1.7
United States	1.5	0.7	0.5	0.5	0.5	0.5	0.5	0.5	0.5	0.5	0.5	0.5
Total exports	9.5	8.9	8.9	8.9	9.0	9.2	9.3	9.4	9.6	9.7	9.8	9.9
					Percent							
U.S. trade share	15.6	7.7	5.9	5.6	5.5	5.2	5.1	5.3	5.5	5.4	5.3	5.2

1/ Covers EU-27, excludes intra-EU trade.
The projections were completed in November 2011.

Table 13. All cotton trade long-term projections

	2010/11	2011/12	2012/13	2013/14	2014/15	2015/16	2016/17	2017/18	2018/19	2019/20	2020/21	2021/22
						Imports, million bales						
Importers												
European Union[1]	1.1	1.0	0.9	0.9	0.9	0.8	0.8	0.8	0.8	0.7	0.7	0.7
Former Soviet Union[2]	0.6	0.6	0.6	0.6	0.6	0.6	0.6	0.6	0.6	0.5	0.5	0.5
Brazil	0.7	0.1	0.2	0.3	0.3	0.3	0.3	0.3	0.3	0.3	0.3	0.3
Mexico	1.2	1.0	1.0	1.1	1.0	1.0	1.0	1.0	1.0	1.0	1.0	1.0
Japan	0.4	0.4	0.4	0.4	0.3	0.3	0.3	0.3	0.3	0.3	0.3	0.3
South Korea	1.0	1.0	1.0	1.0	1.0	1.0	1.0	1.0	1.0	1.0	0.9	0.9
China	12.0	14.0	16.0	16.5	16.5	16.6	16.7	16.8	17.0	17.3	17.6	17.9
Indonesia	2.1	2.3	2.2	2.2	2.2	2.2	2.2	2.2	2.3	2.3	2.3	2.3
Thailand	1.8	1.7	1.7	1.7	1.7	1.7	1.7	1.7	1.7	1.8	1.8	1.8
Pakistan	1.5	1.5	1.5	1.5	1.6	1.7	1.8	1.9	1.9	2.0	2.0	2.1
India	0.5	0.5	0.6	0.6	0.6	0.5	0.5	0.5	0.5	0.5	0.5	0.5
Bangladesh	3.7	3.5	3.4	3.4	3.4	3.5	3.6	3.7	3.8	3.9	4.0	4.2
Taiwan	0.8	0.9	0.8	0.8	0.8	0.8	0.8	0.8	0.8	0.8	0.8	0.7
Other Asia & Oceania	2.3	2.3	2.3	2.3	2.4	2.6	2.7	2.9	3.1	3.3	3.5	3.6
Turkey	3.4	3.1	2.6	2.6	2.5	2.5	2.5	2.5	2.6	2.6	2.6	2.7
Other	2.6	2.5	2.9	3.2	3.3	3.4	3.5	3.7	3.7	3.8	3.9	4.0
Total imports	35.6	36.3	38.1	38.9	39.0	39.5	40.1	40.7	41.4	42.0	42.9	43.6
						Exports, million bales						
Exporters												
Former Soviet Union[2]	4.6	4.6	4.7	4.8	5.1	5.2	5.3	5.4	5.5	5.5	5.5	5.6
Australia	2.5	4.2	4.9	4.2	3.9	3.8	3.7	3.8	3.9	3.9	4.0	4.1
Argentina	0.3	0.2	0.3	0.3	0.3	0.3	0.3	0.4	0.4	0.4	0.4	0.4
Brazil	2.0	3.8	4.0	4.0	4.0	4.1	4.3	4.5	4.7	4.9	5.1	5.4
Other Latin America	0.4	0.3	0.3	0.3	0.3	0.3	0.3	0.4	0.4	0.4	0.4	0.4
Pakistan	0.5	0.5	0.4	0.2	0.2	0.2	0.2	0.2	0.2	0.2	0.2	0.2
India	5.1	5.2	5.0	4.9	4.6	4.4	4.4	4.4	4.5	4.5	4.7	4.8
Egypt	0.4	0.4	0.4	0.4	0.4	0.4	0.4	0.4	0.4	0.4	0.4	0.4
West African Community[3]	2.0	2.2	2.4	2.5	2.6	2.7	2.8	2.9	3.0	3.1	3.3	3.4
Other Sub-Saharan Africa[4]	1.5	1.6	1.5	1.5	1.5	1.6	1.7	1.7	1.8	1.8	1.9	2.0
Other foreign	1.8	2.0	1.9	1.9	1.9	2.0	2.0	2.0	2.0	2.0	2.1	2.1
United States	14.4	11.3	12.4	13.8	14.2	14.5	14.6	14.7	14.7	14.7	14.8	14.8
Total exports	35.6	36.3	38.1	38.9	39.0	39.5	40.1	40.7	41.4	42.0	42.8	43.6
						Percent						
U.S. trade share	40.4	31.1	32.5	35.4	36.5	36.7	36.4	36.1	35.5	35.0	34.6	34.0

1/ Covers EU-27, excludes intra-EU trade.
2/ Covers FSU-12, includes intra-FSU trade.
3/ Economic Community of West African States.
4/ Includes South Africa.
The projections were completed in November 2011.

Table 14. Beef trade long-term projections

	2010	2011	2012	2013	2014	2015	2016	2017	2018	2019	2020	2021
	Imports, thousand metric tons, carcass weight											
Importers												
Japan	721	805	825	854	867	873	875	875	883	888	892	900
South Korea	366	460	485	498	503	513	529	542	559	578	597	617
Taiwan	130	125	125	133	138	141	144	147	150	153	156	159
Philippines	138	145	150	154	157	160	163	166	170	173	176	179
Other Asia	671	782	855	931	980	1,019	1,057	1,097	1,133	1,170	1,211	1,256
European Union[1]	437	370	375	373	371	369	368	366	364	362	360	359
Russia	1,020	1,050	1,060	1,057	1,000	977	986	1,003	1,014	1,024	1,031	1,034
Other Europe	62	68	70	72	73	74	75	75	76	76	76	77
Egypt	260	270	290	302	310	316	323	328	331	333	336	340
Other N. Africa & M. East	920	892	944	1,011	1,060	1,099	1,138	1,175	1,207	1,242	1,276	1,311
Mexico	296	296	308	368	412	425	440	456	489	525	566	599
Canada	243	275	260	262	263	264	270	276	281	285	287	289
United States	1,042	920	948	1,111	1,293	1,345	1,365	1,390	1,417	1,446	1,475	1,504
Major importers	6,306	6,459	6,695	7,126	7,426	7,576	7,732	7,896	8,073	8,254	8,439	8,623
	Exports, thousand metric tons, carcass weight											
Exporters												
Australia	1,368	1,250	1,240	1,260	1,292	1,309	1,313	1,321	1,333	1,338	1,343	1,347
New Zealand	530	501	484	503	522	532	533	533	536	539	544	550
Asia	988	1,182	1,332	1,420	1,508	1,587	1,672	1,755	1,821	1,890	1,962	2,031
European Union[1]	337	475	465	456	449	427	415	419	418	417	417	418
Argentina	298	260	300	273	259	262	266	273	289	299	309	320
Brazil	1,558	1,325	1,298	1,423	1,592	1,654	1,710	1,760	1,806	1,863	1,917	1,971
Canada	523	415	400	404	408	404	402	398	400	405	410	413
United States	1,043	1,254	1,259	1,225	1,236	1,262	1,293	1,321	1,349	1,376	1,404	1,432
Major exporters	6,645	6,662	6,778	6,963	7,266	7,437	7,604	7,780	7,951	8,126	8,304	8,481

1/ Covers EU-27, excludes intra-EU trade.

The projections were completed in November 2011.

Table 15. Pork trade long-term projections

	2010	2011	2012	2013	2014	2015	2016	2017	2018	2019	2020	2021
	Imports, thousand metric tons, carcass weight											
Importers												
Japan	1,198	1,210	1,210	1,210	1,206	1,212	1,209	1,214	1,218	1,220	1,220	1,220
China	415	550	560	635	675	686	705	722	745	766	782	807
Hong Kong	347	360	380	463	472	475	488	495	512	520	540	558
South Korea	382	625	500	499	504	507	514	520	532	539	549	560
Russia	880	930	700	760	720	683	635	600	550	500	445	379
Mexico	687	630	650	670	704	736	776	805	835	865	895	920
Central America/Caribbean	123	110	122	146	161	177	195	215	233	252	270	286
Canada	183	195	190	193	196	199	201	203	205	207	209	210
United States	390	375	370	374	408	431	444	458	472	481	492	503
Major importers	4,605	4,985	4,682	4,949	5,047	5,104	5,166	5,232	5,302	5,350	5,402	5,445
	Exports, thousand metric tons, carcass weight											
Exporters												
Brazil	619	582	570	571	580	590	600	612	624	632	644	658
Canada	1,159	1,160	1,160	1,175	1,192	1,206	1,229	1,247	1,263	1,276	1,286	1,293
Mexico	78	75	75	76	77	78	78	79	80	80	81	81
European Union[1]	1,754	2,000	1,900	1,950	1,995	1,988	1,971	1,954	1,937	1,911	1,885	1,860
China	278	260	280	294	305	319	333	343	353	364	375	383
United States	1,916	2,257	2,309	2,354	2,402	2,449	2,499	2,549	2,599	2,654	2,706	2,760
Major exporters	5,804	6,334	6,294	6,420	6,551	6,630	6,710	6,783	6,856	6,916	6,975	7,035

1/ Covers EU-27, excludes intra-EU trade.

The projections w ere completed in November 2011.

Table 16. Poultry trade long-term projections[1]

	2010	2011	2012	2013	2014	2015	2016	2017	2018	2019	2020	2021
	Imports, thousand metric tons, ready to cook											
Importers												
Russia	668	423	374	254	232	214	197	180	163	146	130	114
European Union[2]	776	790	800	808	816	824	833	841	849	858	866	875
Other Europe	28	35	35	35	35	36	36	36	37	37	37	38
Canada	132	143	143	145	147	149	150	152	153	155	156	158
Mexico	702	760	789	804	814	837	864	882	915	950	979	1,008
Central America/Caribbean	324	276	286	305	320	322	321	324	332	339	348	355
Japan	789	847	805	800	806	805	807	810	812	812	809	809
Hong Kong	295	285	300	316	328	340	353	365	377	390	395	404
China	312	265	295	325	345	358	367	378	386	393	399	407
South Korea	106	130	125	130	134	139	143	146	150	155	159	163
Saudi Arabia	681	830	880	926	950	970	992	1,014	1,036	1,058	1,081	1,106
Other Middle East	1,180	1,316	1,377	1,401	1,440	1,490	1,541	1,592	1,643	1,695	1,748	1,803
North Africa	29	117	147	137	127	122	126	131	136	141	146	152
West African Community[3]	196	260	280	280	303	327	352	382	418	460	502	548
Other Sub-Saharan Africa	427	440	490	506	523	537	567	592	617	643	669	696
Major importers	6,645	6,917	7,126	7,172	7,321	7,469	7,648	7,824	8,023	8,230	8,424	8,634
	Exports, thousand metric tons, ready to cook											
Exporters												
European Union[2]	1,126	1,230	1,250	1,279	1,299	1,317	1,316	1,327	1,327	1,326	1,325	1,329
Brazil	3,339	3,400	3,555	3,620	3,765	3,902	4,074	4,219	4,382	4,538	4,673	4,813
China	379	410	445	442	452	465	481	497	520	544	569	592
Thailand	432	450	500	509	519	531	544	556	574	595	616	636
United States	3,335	3,413	3,413	3,442	3,472	3,502	3,533	3,562	3,593	3,628	3,662	3,697
Major exporters	8,611	8,903	9,163	9,292	9,507	9,717	9,947	10,161	10,396	10,631	10,844	11,067

1/ Broilers and turkeys only.
2/ Covers EU-27, excludes intra-EU trade.
3/ Economic Community of West African States.
The projections were completed in November 2011.